BLUEPRINT

for

Success

POWERHOUSE PROFESSIONALS

14

INSIGHT PUBLISHING

SEVIERVILLE, TENNESSEE

Table of Contents

A Message from the Publisher vii

Margaret Page 1

Stephen R. Covey 13

Frank Prince 27

Suzanne Evans 43

Greg Gillum 57

Julie Maloney 83

Dr. Kenneth Blanchard 97

Sherial Bratcher 113

Deborah George-Feres 131

Ruby Newell-Legner 149

David Coleman 161

Shannon Wallis 181

Bob DeMers 205

Carl Casanova 225

A Message from the Publisher...

When we see the word "blueprint" we usually think of a technical drawing or other image rendered as white lines on a blue background produced by an architect. A blueprint is a detailed plan of action and everyone should develop a blueprint in order to plan for success in life. The men and women in this book have, in interesting and innovative ways, developed their own blueprints that paved the way for their success.

As I interviewed these people, I found that there are as many ways to plan for success, as there are people who create those plans. I was fascinated as I learned from these highly successful people what they did to succeed in their various professions. A successful businesswoman once told me that when she was "involuntarily separated from her last corporate job" she took the opportunity to sit back and take a deep breath, discover what she really wanted to do, and to explore her passion. She said she didn't write anything down but from just taking some time out to think and explore, she came up with her path to success.

At times, successful people have to push through hard times and setbacks. I am always intrigued by the various methods they use to overcome difficulties. Some of them have gone on to teach others what they learned as they went back to the drawing board and created a new blueprint that led them to success.

I believe you will find that your time will be well spent in reading this book. I think you will find that these people have something to say that is worth listening to. I know that I did.

Interviews Conducted by:
David E. Wright, President
International Speakers Network

Chapter One

An interview with…

Margaret Page

David Wright (Wright)

Today we are talking to Margaret Page, the founder and director of Etiquette Page Enterprises, a western Canadian firm offering business etiquette and international protocol services.

With thirty years of success as an entrepreneur and business leader, Ms. Page brings to the table her knowledge and genuine appreciation for the highest standards of etiquette and protocol.

Ms. Page teaches her clients essential skills for handling social situations with style, finesse, and confidence. By applying practical information and sincere advice, they triumph over their competition in domestic and international business arenas.

Ms. Page is privileged to be trained and certified through the prestigious Protocol School of Washington. A believer in ongoing professional development, her education also includes certification in corporate etiquette and international protocol, master level training in Neuro-Linguistic Programming, and advanced level training in Personal and Business Coaching.

Welcome to *Blueprint for Success*.

Margaret Page (Page)

Thank you, David.

Wright

Let me start by asking what the word "etiquette" actually means.

Page

Interestingly enough, the word "etiquette" came about in the court of Louis XIV of France. One of the king's gardeners, who'd just planted new grass, put up a sign that said "e'tiquets," meaning, "keep off the royal lawn" in French. Eventually, the word evolved to mean all the rules of the court, particularly rules for lords and ladies. But of course, having good manners was in vogue long before King Louis's court.

Wright

What is the difference between "etiquette" and "protocol"?

Page

As commonly applied in diplomatic circles, protocol refers to black-and-white behavior while etiquette has shades of gray. Think of protocol as being a precise set of guidelines and rules, much like the ones that computers have to follow. Etiquette carries some flexibility with it.

Wright

When did we as a society start being interested in good manners?

Page

About 2500 BC. That's when the first recorded documentation about good manners appeared. An Egyptian pharaoh's scholar had written a book of guidelines titled *Instructions of Ptah-hotep* for his son on how young men should behave in order to climb the social ladder. It outlined principles of considerate human relations. One recommendation was that if a superior laughs, the young social climber should laugh as well. (That might still be good advice today.)

Since the time of the Egyptian pharaohs, etiquette has ebbed and flowed in its popularity. Good manners seem to gain prominence when we experience mass changes in how we behave as a people. That's when manners get written down on paper and are shared with people in the community as a whole.

During the Renaissance period, for example, a great Dutch philosopher and scholar named Erasmus wrote that if young people were trained in etiquette, the world would be a better place. He believed in the importance of instilling manners at an early age and wrote *De civilitate morum puerilium (A Little Book of Good Manners for Children)*, a book that continued to be reprinted well into the eighteenth century. In fact, it spawned a multitude of translations, imitations, and sequels.

The subject of etiquette was also on everyone's lips just after the First World War—the era of Emily Post. That's when cars and movies were new in society. When it came to knowing how to behave politely, everyone was asking, "What would Emily Post say?"

Today, that desire is building again because of the Internet, cell phones, telecommunications, and globalization. This technology is bringing together people from so many different countries. They crave information on how to treat each other when using modern-day tools, especially cell phones and PDAs, which can be rudely intrusive.

You've seen it happen. You're talking with someone and that person's cell phone rings. You stand idle while he or she carries on a conversation. It's like conveying the message to you that "you're not the most important person to me right now."

Or someone near you fails to find a private place and use a "library" voice when speaking on a cell phone. It distracts you from your own conversation, so you politely say, "Can you please move to another location to carry on your conversation? We're unable to talk because of your voice." Now, if you can't say something like this politely, then move away from the person—no sense responding to one rude act with another: two rudes never make a right.

Wright

Considering we live in a global community now, how has etiquette changed over time?

3

Page

We've become much more understanding and accepting of other people's customs in our global village. We're more willing to embrace those customs and share in them than ever before. If you are visiting other countries and don't behave correctly, the natives are tolerant of it. In fact, they don't expect you to behave perfectly. However, they're clearly pleased when you attempt to use their language and gestures, their styles of eating, and their forms of communicating with each other.

Wright

Ms. Page, how does our increasingly global society impact good manners and etiquette? Culturally, are there great differences in the way we interact with each other that affect our manners?

Page

I think that, over time, our society has gained flexibility and we willingly embrace other people's styles of dining and greeting. We enjoy learning new things—including new manners—when we visit countries that are fresh and different to us.

As an example, a number of years ago I had the opportunity to visit China. There, I learned that when you're part of an intimate group dining together, you adopt this interesting custom: When a bowl of food comes to you on a serving platter, you first put some food on the plate of the person to your left and then you put some food on the plate of the person on your right. Finally, you put food on your own plate.

It's a way to be more observant of what those beside you need, what they actually eat, and how they like to enjoy their meals. I loved doing that in China because it added a sense of mindfulness and respect. We have so many worthwhile things to learn from people in other countries and we can use them to improve our day-to-day lives.

Wright

When and how did you become interested in etiquette, Ms. Page?

Page

When I was six years old, I was invited out for dinner for the first time ever without my parents. I went with my older brother, who was in grade six at that time. I'd always looked up to him as my hero. As we walked over to our neighbor's house for dinner, he said sternly, "Now, Margaret, don't you embarrass me." I shook with fear that I'd do something wrong!

When we got there, I noticed foods on the table I'd never seen before: shrimp that I didn't know how to deal with and asparagus, a vegetable I'd never eaten before. Mostly, I thought these people were absolutely amazing because they had put grapes on the table. I couldn't wait to get home and tell Mom these people actually ate grapes for dinner! I wanted to do it too. So I put two or three "grapes" on my plate to eat a bit later. At one point, I decided to enjoy one and popped it into my mouth, only to discover a hugely awful taste. It sure didn't taste like a grape! I had never come in contact with an olive before and didn't know which way to turn.

I never wanted to experience that awkward feeling again myself. And since then, I never wanted others to feel uncomfortable when dining out either. Being with people should be pleasurable and not uncomfortable, no matter what era, age, or culture.

A few years after that awkward, uncomfortable dinner, I read a marketing piece about the Book of the Month Club featuring Emily Post's *Book of Etiquette*. I pleaded with my parents to sign up for the Book of the Month Club so I could get this book. I was only ten years old. And four decades later, I still own that book. I've referred to it hundreds of times throughout the years.

Wright

That was a great story. I thought you were going to say that the grapes turned out to be made of wax!

Page

That reminds of a time I was teaching a program and an attendee shared his eating experience on an airline. He did not realize there was wax on the cheese. He popped one in this mouth and got wax all over his teeth. Unfortunately, he had to refrain from further conversation, wait until the aisles were clear, and excuse himself to take care of the matter in the restroom. I certainly empathized with him.

Wright

What is your biggest challenge teaching etiquette?

Page

Etiquette consultants are faced with the myth that their guidelines all start with, "Thou shalt not do this." It conjures up an image of a prim woman standing over us and shaking her finger. That image leaves a negative feeling and perception toward the whole subject of manners.

But think of the fact that we live in an era of human potential. We're encouraged to focus on the positive and what does work—not what doesn't. That requires dropping edicts like, "Thou shalt not put your elbows on the table" and instead, giving positive suggestions for good manners like, "When resting at the table, place your hands on your lap." Or instead of the edict, "Don't talk with your mouth full," you could say, "If you have something to share in the way of words, please do so after you've finished chewing your food."

People really do want to embrace guidelines and move forward with them, instead of reacting negatively and thinking, "Oh, do I have to learn this?" That's where etiquette training comes in.

Wright

I've heard you talk about MQ or Manners Quotient. Could you tell us what that is?

Page

With the Manners Quotient or MQ, if you handle things related to manners effectively, then you earn a high MQ score.

Wright

Does that mean there's a test?

Page

Yes. I selected five items for this MQ quiz because the word "manners" is derived from the Spanish word "manus" or "hand." In common usage, "manners" means "to handle." So just like we have five fingers on a hand, we have these five questions:

1. Have you taken etiquette training or read an etiquette-training book in the last ten years? (If yes, give yourself 1 point.)
2. When you observe how others behave, do you regard their behavior as a tool to guide your own behavior rather than judge them? (If yes, give yourself 2 points.)
3. Do you make a person you speak with feel like he or she is the most important person in the room? Related to that, do you refrain from talking on your cell phone when others are present? (If yes to both, give yourself 2 points.)
4. Are you kind to others and "good-mouth" (rather than bad-mouth) them? (If yes, give yourself 2 points.) This rule embraces much more than the golden rule, which is "to do unto others as you would have them do unto you." It helps make people feel good about themselves.
5. Do you respect, honor, and accept people from cultures other than your own? As you travel and interact with them, do you take time to learn about their culture and make strong connections? (If yes to all, give yourself 3 points.)

If you scored 8 to 10 points, you've got a head start on connecting well with others. If you scored 4 to 7 points, pay attention; there's more you can learn. If you scored 3 or fewer points, make a commitment to apply good manners in every situation possible. For assistance, you can refer to the resources on my Web site at www.etiquettepage.com. Specifically look for the Cognito Cards, which spell out considerate behavior choices using easy reference cards.

Wright

Do you have any etiquette tips you can share right now?

Page

Here's a quick tip: When you go to a cocktail party, hold your beverage in your left hand so your right hand is free from moisture. This also makes it easy to shake hands with people.

Wright

I'm always afraid my hand will be cold because I've been holding a glass of iced tea or coke. This is a good idea!

Page

Think of it this way: Once you feel comfortable using your left hand for your drink, you free your right hand to welcome new people into your life.

Here's another tip: If you're at an event and have a nametag, wear it on your right shoulder, not your left. As you shift to shake hands and greet a new person, you'll naturally shift to the left. When that person responds to your handshake, he or she can immediately read the nametag because it's on your right shoulder. You'll also find people remember your name better when you wear your nametag on the right.

Wright

When you get right down to it, etiquette is not so much trying to do things with pomp and ceremony, but it's about being practical, like the two examples you just gave me, right?

Page

Absolutely. Once you understand the rules of the road for driving, then driving becomes easier. It's the same when applied to relating to others in social settings. Knowing the rules of the road for dining and social etiquette makes life flow more easily. Instead of being concerned about doing things properly, you can focus on building relationships or discussing the matters at hand. A lot of etiquette is really common sense.

Wright

What etiquette questions do you get asked most often?

Page

Here's the most common one: Say you're dining out in a group. When the bill arrives, who pays? Someone always pipes up and says, "I don't eat as much the rest of the others. Do I have to pay as much?"

The guideline for dining out is this: If you've extended the invitation for others to join you, then you're the host and you take care of paying the bill. But I realize there's not always a designated host. When I lived in Las Vegas, I knew a gentleman named Tex, a controller in the U.S. Navy, who was highly skilled at math. When we'd go out to dinner with ten or twelve people in our wine-tasting group, Tex would track what everyone drank and ate in his head. The waitperson would bring the bill to him and he'd pass around a note telling each person the amount owed, tip included. He did it so seamlessly, we never had to spend time dividing things up.

One night while dining out with Tex, I ordered a steak, the special for the evening. When the bill came, I saw Tex pointing to me while speaking to the waiter. Later, I asked if there had been a problem. He told me the waiter had billed an incorrect amount for the steak. I thought, "Wow! Tex was looking out for me and I didn't even know it!" I certainly recommend finding a "Tex" in your group who will make it easy for everyone. Now, if you can't find someone like Tex, I suggest dividing the bill as quietly as possible and paying your fair share. If the process repeatedly proves awkward or uncomfortable, then find different friends to dine out with!

Wright

I used to dine with several couples and a few people in the group would order appetizers and expensive wine, then we'd all split the bill. Some in the group didn't like this because they didn't drink wine or eat appetizers. We solved this dilemma by doing what you suggested—going with out different friends who didn't order appetizers and wine.

Page

I remember dining out with a group one evening and having a lovely time. The conversation was delightful, the food was stupendous, and the wine was the final polish to a fabulous meal. We didn't mind that it was an expensive evening; when the bill came, everyone just threw in their money to cover it. But we came up about $60 short. I quickly threw a $20 bill on the table, but no one else was coming up with extra cash. I wondered if I'd have to contribute even more money, but after a long, difficult silence, the others finally put in enough to cover the shortfall.

On the way home that night, I thought, "What a shame to have my memories of that lovely evening scarred by making paying the bill a thorny issue." The experience tended to ruin our sense of fair play, which is really what makes people feel good about each other.

Wright

I have seen men and women lose jobs over questions of etiquette. They were up for promotions that required a lot of dining out with customers. But they had such poor manners, they were passed over for those who not only had good manners but knew protocol as well.

Page

Studies have shown that 45 percent of workers leave their jobs because they felt they were treated rudely at work. A combined study described in *Academy of Management Executiv*, noted that "uncivility" or rudeness leads to one out of eight people leaving their jobs. *In extreme cases, it can end up in aggressive behavior in the workplace.* Certainly loss of income is an undesirable result.

A study by Public Agenda and published in *TIME* magazine (among others) indicates that eight out of ten Americans believe a lack of courtesy is a serious problem for society today. Of those surveyed, 66 percent said they were bothered "a lot" by reckless drivers and 56 percent stated they were annoyed by people who use vulgar language in public.

These studies show that poor etiquette isn't a trivial problem in our society. On the positive side, they indicate having excellent manners makes you more memorable to others.

Think back to various stages of your life and several people will stand out in your mind simply because they were well mannered. When it's time to choose someone to speak at a conference or start a friendship with or invite to a party, we remember them. Here's an example.

Four years ago, as a passenger on a ferry, I was walking toward a stairway when I saw a boy about six years old holding open a heavy door for his mom. This young gentleman continued to hold the door for me while I climbed about eight steps. When I sincerely thanked him for taking time to do that, he said, "You're very welcome, madam," in a way that showed full respect for me. I smiled inside and I'm still smiling because I remember this incident so well. I remember his clothing, his hair, and his considerate tone of voice. Mostly I remember that his kind action made me feel honored as a person. In less than a minute, he left an impression that will last all my life—and gave me hope that good manners will thrive well into the future.

About Margaret Page...

Margaret Page is the founder and director of Etiquette Page Enterprises, a western Canadian firm offering business etiquette and international protocol services. With 30 years of success as an entrepreneur and business leader, Ms. Page brings to her clients proven knowledge and genuine appreciation for the highest standards of etiquette and protocol. Ms. Page inspires her clients, giving them the essential skills and confidence required to handle any situation they encounter with style and finesse. Using practical information and sincere advice, her clients outclass and triumph over the competition in domestic and international business arena.

Ms. Page is privileged to be trained and certified by the prestigious Protocol School of Washington®. Her broad educational background spans informal and formal studies, with certification in corporate etiquette and international protocol, master level training in Neuro-Linguistic Programming, and advanced level training in Personal and Business Coaching.

As a dynamic trainer, Ms. Page has delivered dozens of seminars and briefings throughout her career. She conducts inspiring programs and private consultations, custom designing interactive sessions based on her clients' needs. She provides a roadmap for them to find answers to their questions, expertly and compassionately walking them through real-life business and social scenarios. She helps them build their social savvy, so they can enter any room or occasion with confidence and grace. Her genuine interest in her students and expertise in etiquette and protocol make Ms. Page an accommodating and informative teacher and role model.

Margaret Page, Founder and Director
Etiquette Page Enterprises
1489 Marine Drive, Suite 411
West Vancouver, BC V7T 1B8
604.880.8002
etiquettepage@aol.com
www.etiquettepage.com

Chapter Two

An interview with...

Stephen R. Covey

David Wright (Wright)

We're talking today with Dr. Stephen R. Covey, cofounder and vice-chairman of Franklin Covey Company, the largest management company and leadership development organization in the world. Dr. Covey is perhaps best known as author of The 7 Habits of Highly Effective People which is ranked as a number one best-seller by the New York Times, having sold more than fourteen million copies in thirty-eight languages throughout the world. Dr. Covey is an internationally respected leadership authority, family expert, teacher, and organizational consultant. He has made teaching principle-centered living and principle-centered leadership his life's work. Dr. Covey is the recipient of the Thomas More College Medallion for Continuing Service to Humanity and has been awarded four honorary doctorate degrees. Other awards given Dr. Covey include the Sikh's 1989 International Man of Peace award, the 1994 International Entrepreneur of the Year award, Inc. magazine's Services Entrepreneur of the Year award, and in 1996 the National Entrepreneur of the Year Lifetime Achievement award for Entrepreneurial leadership. He has also been recognized as one of Time magazine's twenty-five most influential Americans and one of Sales and Marketing Management's top twenty-five power brokers. As the father of nine and grandfather of forty-four, Dr. Covey received the 2003 National Fatherhood Award, which he says is the most meaningful award he has ever received. Dr. Covey earned his undergraduate degree from the University of Utah, his MBA from Harvard, and completed his doctorate at Brigham Young University. While at Brigham Young he served as assistant to the President and was also a professor of Business Management and Organizational Behavior.

Dr. Covey, welcome to *Blueprint for Success*.

Dr. Stephen Covey (Covey)

Thank you.

Wright

Dr. Covey, most companies make decisions and filter them down through their organization. You, however, state that no company can succeed until individuals within it succeed. Are the goals of the company the result of the combined goals of the individuals?

Covey

Absolutely—if people aren't on the same page, they're going to be pulling in different directions. To teach this concept, I frequently ask large audiences to close their eyes and point north, and then to keep pointing and open their eyes. They find themselves pointing all over the place. I say to them, "Tomorrow morning if you want a similar experience, ask the first ten people you meet in your organization what the purpose of your organization is and you'll find it's a very similar experience. They'll point all over the place." When people have a different sense of purpose and values, every decision that is made from then on is governed by those. There's no question that this is one of the fundamental causes of misalignment, low trust, interpersonal conflict, interdepartmental rivalry, people operating on personal agendas, and so forth.

Wright

Is that primarily a result of an inability to communicate from the top?

Covey

That's one aspect, but I think it's more fundamental. There's an inability to involve people—an unwillingness. Leaders may communicate what their mission and their strategy is, but that doesn't mean there's any emotional connection to it. Mission statements that are rushed and then announced are soon forgotten. They become nothing more than just a bunch of platitudes on the wall that mean essentially nothing and even create a source of cynicism and a sense of hypocrisy inside the culture of an organization.

Wright

How do companies ensure survival and prosperity in these tumultuous times of technological advances, mergers, downsizing, and change?

Covey

I think that it takes a lot of high trust in a culture that has something that doesn't change—principles—at its core. There are principles that people agree upon that are valued. It gives a sense of stability. Then you have the power to adapt and be flexible when you experience these kinds of disruptive new economic models or technologies that come in and sideswipe you. You don't know how to handle them unless you have something you can depend upon.

If people have not agreed to a common set of principles that guide them and a common purpose, then they get their security from the outside and they tend to freeze the structure, systems, and processes inside and they cease becoming adaptable. They don't change with the changing realities of the new marketplace out there and gradually they become obsolete.

Wright

I was interested in one portion of your book, The 7 Habits of Highly Effective People, where you talk about behaviors. How does an individual go about the process of replacing ineffective behaviors with effective ones?

Covey

I think that for most people it usually requires a crisis that humbles them to become aware of their ineffective behaviors. If there's not a crisis the tendency is to perpetuate those behaviors and not change.

You don't have to wait until the marketplace creates the crisis for you. Have everyone accountable on a 360 degree basis to everyone else they interact with—

with feedback either formal or informal—where they are getting data as to what's happening. They will then start to realize that the consequences of their ineffective behavior require them to be humble enough to look at that behavior and to adopt new, more effective ways of doing things.

Sometimes people can be stirred up to this if you just appeal to their conscience—to their inward sense of what is right and wrong. A lot of people sometimes know inwardly they're doing wrong, but the culture doesn't necessarily discourage them from continuing that. They either need feedback from people or they need feedback from the marketplace or they need feedback from their conscience. Then they can begin to develop a step-by-step process of replacing old habits with new, better habits.

Wright

It's almost like saying, "Let's make all the mistakes in the laboratory before we put this thing in the air."

Covey

Right; and I also think what is necessary is a paradigm shift, which is analogous to having a correct map, say of a city or of a country. If people have an inaccurate paradigm of life, of other people, and of themselves it really doesn't make much difference what their behavior or habits or attitudes are. What they need is a correct paradigm—a correct map—that describes what's going on.

For instance, in the Middle Ages they used to heal people through bloodletting. It wasn't until Samuel Weiss and Pasteur and other empirical scientists discovered the germ theory that they realized for the first time they weren't dealing with the real issue. They realized why women preferred to use midwives who washed rather than doctors who didn't wash. They gradually got a new paradigm. Once you've got a new paradigm then your behavior and your attitude flows directly from it. If you have a bad paradigm or a bad map, let's say of a city, there's no way, no matter what your behavior or your habits or your attitudes are—how positive they are—you'll never be able to find the location you're looking for. This is why I believe that to change paradigms is far more fundamental than to work on attitude and behavior.

Wright

One of your seven habits of highly effective people is to "begin with the end in mind." If circumstances change and hardships or miscalculation occurs, how does one view the end with clarity?

Covey

Many people think to begin with the end in mind means that you have some fixed definition of a goal that's accomplished and if changes come about you're not going to adapt to them. Instead, the "end in mind" you begin with is that you are going to create a flexible culture of high trust so that no matter what comes along you are going to do whatever it takes to accommodate that new change or that new reality and maintain a culture of high performance and high trust. You're talking more in terms of values and overall purposes that don't change, rather than specific strategies or programs that will have to change to accommodate the changing realities in the marketplace.

Wright

In this time of mistrust between people, corporations, and nations for that matter, how do we create high levels of trust?

Covey

That's a great question and it's complicated because there are so many elements that go into the creating of a culture of trust. Obviously the most fundamental one is just to have trustworthy people. But that is not sufficient because what if the organization itself is misaligned?

For instance, what if you say you value cooperation but you really reward people for internal competition? Then you have a systemic or a structure problem that creates low trust inside the culture even though the people themselves are trustworthy. This is one of the insights of Edward Demming and the work he did.

That's why he said that most problems are not personal—they're systemic. They're common caused. That's why you have to work on structure, systems, and processes to make sure that they institutionalize principle-centered values. Otherwise you could have good people with bad systems and you'll get bad results.

When it comes to developing interpersonal trust between people, it is made up of many, many elements such as taking the time to listen to other people, to understand them, and to see what is important to them. What we think is important to another may only be important to us, not to another. It takes empathy. You have to make and keep promises to them. You have to treat people with kindness and courtesy. You have to be completely honest and open. You have to live up to your commitments. You can't betray people behind their back. You can't badmouth them behind their back and sweet-talk them to their face. That will send out vibes of hypocrisy and it will be detected.

You have to learn to apologize when you make mistakes, to admit mistakes, and to also get feedback going in every direction as much as possible. It doesn't necessarily require formal forums—it requires trust between people who will be open with each other and give each other feedback.

Wright

My mother told me to do a lot of what you're saying now, but it seems that when I got in business I simply forgot.

Covey

Sometimes we forget, but sometimes culture doesn't nurture it. That's why I say unless you work with the institutionalizing—that means formalizing into structure, systems, and processes the values—you will not have a nurturing culture. You have to constantly work on that.

This is one of the big mistakes organizations make. They think trust is simply a function of being honest. That's only one small aspect. It's an important aspect, obviously, but there are so many other elements that go into the creation of a high trust culture.

Wright

"Seek first to understand then to be understood" is another of your seven habits. Do you find that people try to communicate without really understanding what other people want?

Covey

Absolutely. The tendency is to project out of our own autobiography—our own life, our own value system—onto other people, thinking we know what they want. So we don't really listen to them. We pretend to listen, but we really don't listen from within their frame of reference. We listen from within our own frame of reference and we're really preparing our reply rather than seeking to understand. This is a very common thing. In fact, very few people have had any training in seriously listening. They're trained in how to read, write, and speak, but not to listen.

Reading, writing, speaking, and listening are the four modes of communication and they represent about two-thirds to three-fourths of our waking hours. About half of that time is spent listening, but it's the one skill people have not been trained in. People have had all this training in the other forms of communication. In a large audience of 1,000 people you wouldn't have more than twenty people who have had more than two weeks of training in listening. Listening is more than a skill or a technique so that you're listening within another frame of reference. It takes tremendous courage to listen because you're at risk when you listen. You don't know what's going to happen; you're vulnerable.

Wright

Sales gurus always tell me that the number one skill in selling is listening.

Covey

Yes—listening from within the customer's frame of reference. That is so true. You can see that it takes some security to do that because you don't know what's going to happen.

Wright

With this book we're trying to encourage people to be better, to live better, and be more fulfilled by listening to the examples of our guest authors. Is there anything or anyone in your life that has made a difference for you and helped you to become a better person?

Covey

I think the most influential people in my life have been my parents. I think that what they modeled was not to make comparisons and harbor jealousy or to seek recognition. They were humble people.

I remember one time when my mother and I were going up in an elevator and the most prominent person in the state was also in the elevator. She knew him, but she spent her time talking to the elevator operator. I was just a little kid and I was so awed by the famous person. I said to her, "Why didn't you talk to the important person?" She said, "I was. I had never met him."

My parents were really humble, modest people who were focused on service and other people rather than on themselves. I think they were very inspiring models to me.

Wright

In almost every research paper I've ever read, those who write about people who have influenced their lives, among the top five people include three teachers. My seventh grade English teacher was the greatest teacher I ever had and she influenced me to no end.

Covey

Would it be correct to say that she saw in you probably some qualities of greatness you didn't even see in yourself?

Wright

Absolutely.

Covey

That's been my general experience—the key aspect of a mentor or a teacher is someone who sees in you potential that you don't even see in yourself. Those teachers/mentors treat you accordingly and eventually you come to see it in yourself. That's my definition of leadership or influence—communicating people's worth and potential so clearly that they are inspired to see it in themselves.

Wright

Most of my teachers treated me as a student, but she treated me with much more respect than that. As a matter of fact, she called me Mr. Wright, and I was in the seventh grade at the time. I'd never been addressed by anything but a nickname. I stood a little taller; she just made a tremendous difference.

Do you think there are other characteristics that mentors seem to have in common?

Covey

I think they are first of all good examples in their own personal lives. Their personal lives and their family lives are not all messed up—they come from a base of good character. They also are usually very confident and they take the time to do what your teacher did to you—to treat you with uncommon respect and courtesy.

They also, I think, explicitly teach principles rather than practices so that rules don't take the place of human judgment. You gradually come to have faith in your own judgment in making decisions because of the affirmation of such a mentor. Good mentors care about you—you can feel the sincerity of their caring. It's like the expression, "I don't care how much you know until I know how much you care."

Wright

Most people are fascinated with the new television shows about being a survivor. What has been the greatest comeback that you've made from adversity in your career or your life?

Covey

When I was in grade school I experienced a disease in my legs. It caused me to use crutches for a while. I tried to get off them fast and get back. The disease wasn't corrected yet so I went back on crutches for another year. The disease went to the other leg and I went on for another year. It essentially took me out of my favorite thing—athletics—and it took me more into being a student. So that was a life-defining experience, which at the time seemed very negative, but has proven to be the basis on which I've focused my life—being more of a learner.

Wright

Principle-centered learning is basically what you do that's different from anybody I've read or listened to.

Covey

The concept is embodied in the far-eastern expression, "Give a man a fish, you feed him for the day; teach him how to fish, you feed him for a lifetime." When you teach principles that are universal and timeless, they don't belong to just any one person's religion or to a particular culture or geography. They seem to be timeless and universal like the ones we've been talking about here: trustworthiness, honesty, caring, service, growth, and development. These are universal principles. If you focus on these things, then little by little people become independent of you and then they start to believe in themselves and their own judgment becomes better. You don't need as many rules. You don't need as much bureaucracy and as many controls and you can empower people.

The problem in most business operations today—and not just business but non-business—is that they're using the industrial model in an information age. Arnold Toynbee, the great historian, said, "You can pretty well summarize all of history in four words: nothing fails like success." The industrial model was based on the asset of the machine. The information model is based on the asset of the person—the knowledge worker. It's an altogether different model. But the machine model was the main asset of the twentieth century. It enabled productivity to increase fifty times. The new asset is intellectual and social capital—

the qualities of people and the quality of the relationship they have with each other. Like Toynbee said, "Nothing fails like success." The industrial model does not work in an information age. It requires a focus on the new wealth, not capital and material things.

A good illustration that demonstrates how much we were into the industrial model, and still are, is to notice where people are on the balance sheet. They're not found there. Machines are found there. Machines become investments. People are on the profit and loss statement and people are expenses. Think of that—if that isn't bloodletting.

Wright

It sure is.

When you consider the choices you've made down through the years, has faith played an important role in your life?

Covey

It has played an extremely important role. I believe deeply that we should put principles at the center of our lives, but I believe that God is the source of those principles. I did not invent them. I get credit sometimes for some of the Seven Habits material and some of the other things I've done, but it's really all based on principles that have been given by God to all of His children from the beginning of time. You'll find that you can teach these same principles from the sacred texts and the wisdom literature of almost any tradition. I think the ultimate source of that is God and that is one thing you can absolutely depend upon—"in God we trust."

Wright

If you could have a platform and tell our audience something you feel would help them or encourage them, what would you say?

Covey

I think I would say to put God at the center of your life and then prioritize your family. No one on their deathbed ever wished they had spent more time at the office.

Wright

That's right. We have come down to the end of our program and I know you're a busy person. I could talk with you all day, Dr. Covey.

Covey

It's good to talk with you as well and to be a part of this program. It looks like an excellent one that you've got going on here.

Wright

Thank you.

We have been talking today with Dr. Stephen R. Covey, co-founder and vice-chairman of Franklin Covey Company. He's also the author of The 7 Habits of Highly Effective People, which has been ranked as a number one bestseller by the New York Times, selling more than fourteen million copies in thirty-eight languages.

Dr. Covey, thank you so much for being with us today.

Covey

Thank you for the honor of participating.

About Stephen R. Covey...

STEPHEN R. COVEY was recognized in 1996 as one of Time magazine's twenty-five most influential Americans and one of Sales and Marketing Management's top twenty-five power brokers. Dr. Covey is the author of several ac-claimed books, including the international bestseller, The 7 Habits of Highly Effective People, named the number one Most Influential Business Book of the Twentieth Century, and other best sellers that include First Things First, Principle-Centered Leadership, (with sales exceeding one million) and The 7 Habits of Highly Effective Families.

Dr. Covey's newest book, The 8th Habit: From Effectiveness to Greatness, which was released in November 2004, rose to the top of several bestseller lists, including New York Times, Wall Street Journal, USA Today, Money, Business Week, Amazon.com, and Barnes & Noble.

Dr. Covey earned his undergraduate degree from the University of Utah, his MBA from Harvard, and completed his doctorate at Brigham Young University. While at Brigham Young University, he served as assistant to the President and was also a professor of Business Management and Organizational Behavior. He received the National Fatherhood Award in 2003, which, as the father of nine and grandfather of forty-four, he says is the most meaningful award he has ever received.

Dr. Covey currently serves on the board of directors for the Points of Light Foundation. Based in Washington, D.C., the Foundation, through its partnership with the Volunteer Center National Network, engages and mobilizes millions of volunteers from all walks of life—businesses, nonprofits, faith-based organizations, low-income communities, families, youth, and older adults—to help solve serious social problems in thousands of communities.

Dr. Stephen R. Covey
www.stephencovey.com

Chapter Three

An interview with...

Frank Prince

David Wright (Wright)

Frank A. Prince is the President and Founder of Unleash Your Mind, a consulting firm whose goal is to unlock innovative thinking within organizations. His expertise lies in motivating people to *stop talking about it* and *start doing it.* Frank is recognized as a global leader in the field of creativity. A popular keynote speaker, he travels the world sparking innovation in organizations and individuals. He is the author of seven books. His bestseller, *C & the Box,* a parable of innovation in business, has been made into an animated video. By conducting skill-building workshops in Creative Problem-Solving, Customer-Focused Selling, and Leadership Development, Frank transforms businesses into "idea factories." He also facilitates Strategic Planning sessions with top executive teams. These sessions focus on driving top and bottom line growth over the ensuing year through implementation of innovation.

Frank has focused his energy on understanding creativity at a subconscious level and has created two products targeted at the subconscious mind. *Speed Sleep* is an audio recording that both accelerates sleep and jump-starts the brain's incubation process. This incubation process can help us solve problems literally while we sleep. *Thought-Free Golf* is an instructional book and CD system that provides the skills to master the mental side of the game of golf.

Frank, welcome to *Blueprint for Success.*

You consider creativity and innovation strategies key to success and survival for businesses in the future. Will you tell us why?

Frank Prince (Prince)

Today we are forced to deal with a rapidly accelerating rate of change. We all feel the pressure of keeping up with the latest technologies. These technologies affect every area of our lives from the self-check at our local grocery to our company issued "PDAs." Every day, sometimes even every hour, there are new skills we need to learn to keep up with the constantly changing world around us. The key to being able to function in the midst of all this change is *adaptability*. This is especially true in business. Companies that can adapt quickly will move forward. Those who hesitate, even a moment, will falter and be left behind.

Consumers' habits are evolving. They are becoming less loyal and more willing to try other brands. There is barely a pause prior to switching brands if a customer comes to believe that a new product will meet their needs as adequately or better than what they usually buy.

Today's businesses need to create an environment that allows and even encourages innovation and adaptation. Organizations cannot get locked into established systems. The very systems that led them to success in the past can lead them into a downward spiral if they are not willing to examine and reinvent them.

I truly believe that there is a direct correlation between a company's success rate and its culture of innovation. A culture of innovation supports and rewards employees who are willing to initiate and complete positive change.

Wright

So businesses need to become more innovative. How do they make innovation a part of their culture?

Prince

Culture changes begin with the individual. A new business culture can be scary and let's face it, it can take more effort to move on than to do things the way they have always been done. But if employees are taught and encouraged to utilize creative thinking skills, true innovation will follow and the results can be exciting.

We are all born creative. Unfortunately, over time, people tend to stop using this inborn creativity. We are taught in school to look for single solutions to our problems. We are taught to look for the "right" answer instead of being open to multiple ideas. Highly creative adults have found a way to continue to use the creative thinking skills that are common to all of us when we are young.

The human brain has four key functions:

- The ability to absorb or take in information
- The ability to take that information and store it
- The ability to recall or pull that information out
- The ability to evaluate the information that the brain has stored

Every moment of every day our brain is absorbing information and organizing it into memories. True innovation comes from the ability to create a quantity of options. To do this we have to be able to pull the stored information back out of our brains in large quantities or lists.

Successful implementation of creativity within an organization requires individuals with the ability to generate a large enough quantity of information to get to a quality of facts and ideas. This listing of information and ideas is called "divergent thinking."

I work with artists who want their work to be unique but find it hard to create quantity at that exceptional level. But to be financially successful they need to be able to create a quantity of their art form, whatever that is. The creativity skill of divergent thinking is the key to being able to create uniqueness in quantity. The only other way to keep from being a "starving artist" is to die, thereby creating uniqueness through scarcity (and death isn't really a desirable strategy to say the least!).

The biggest obstacle to divergent thinking in business is the fear of losing the logic that comes with the use of evaluation skills. To be truly divergent you have to be willing to set aside evaluation and defer judgment. However, a divergent list of options, no matter how creative, is not useful until a viable choice is made from that list. That's where the evaluation skills that we have developed over the years come in. The trick is to be able to set all our experience and judgment aside just long enough to develop a long list of creative options to choose from.

Another key creativity principle is the ability to shift perspective or to look at things differently. Organizations can get locked into seeing things a certain way because that is what their experience has been for so many years. Experience, though valuable, begins to blind them to options. That is why bringing in a new person can often help a company alter its point of view.

If divergent thought and the ability to shift perspective are valued in the workplace the culture can be changed to a more innovative and creative one. The key to moving toward true innovation is to value the principles of creative thought that make it possible.

Wright

What stops us from being more innovative in the workplace?

Prince

In our growing out of the naturally creative children we once were we develop a number of habits that can stifle our creativity as adults. In school we are taught to find the "right" answer. In fact, we are graded on our ability to find the single correct solution to the problems we are given. We transfer that habit to the workplace. When presented with a business challenge we naturally look for the "right" answer. By doing this we begin immediately narrowing our choices. When searching for that single correct solution we are convergent in thought. Breaking the habit of looking for the one right answer is one of the biggest challenges to becoming more creative at work or in our personal lives.

The environment where ideas are shared and received is another thing that can affect innovation in the workplace. Often, when an idea is presented it is immediately evaluated and critiqued. For ideas to grow into valuable innovations they have to be given a chance. Sharing an idea at work is a risk. A person who is willing to take that risk has to feel passionate about it. Judging that idea too quickly not only stops the whole creative process but can also shut down an enthusiastic employee. For a new idea to be fostered it has to be built on by others in the organization, not immediately stomped into the ground. Organizations need a methodology for enhancing or adding to ideas.

Sometimes making successful changes in the business culture is as simple as breaking these habitual ways of approaching thought and ideas and fostering an environment that rewards individuals who think differently.

Wright

Many organizations have "brainstorming sessions," is this what you are talking about?

Prince

The classic "brainstorming session," involves getting people together and making a big list. There is a lot of energy and it can be fun but what generally ends up happening is that someone takes the list back, folds it, and puts it in a drawer somewhere. Most "brainstorming" ends with enthusiastic inaction. People tell me about a brainstorming session where some terrific ideas were discussed but nobody did a single thing with them. The problem with just brainstorming is that more often than not there is no application. For businesses to be truly successful they need "applied creativity"—creative ideas taken to action. Applied creativity requires both divergent and convergent thought and a willingness to look at things from a new perspective.

When I speak I make a distinction between creativity, invention, and innovation. Creativity is a novel thought or idea. Invention is a novel thought or idea in tangible form. Innovation is a novel thought or idea in a tangible form that is used for some type of a gain. That gain can be dollars and cents or can come in some other form, but an innovation always results in gain. The successful business is able to move creativity all the way to innovation. By using applied creativity the "brainstorming session" can be taken to application through an action plan that implements the ideas.

Truly innovative organizations are "idea factories" where big ideas are not just talked about but are put into action. These companies are constantly coming up with ideas, evaluating them, and putting the best of them in place.

Wright

So how do you create an "idea factory"?

Prince

It is common for organizations to have a group of people who are seen as the "creatives." Sometimes research and development is put in this role.

In an organization that is truly an "idea factory" every person is active in idea development and implementation. Every employee has the ability to transform what he or she does each day. All the employees have the ability to change their small parts of the business by making them better or more efficient. The smart employer looks at each individual as a resource. In the "idea factory" every worker is encouraged to come up with viable ideas and is empowered to implement them.

It is a powerful truth that people support what they help to create. Employees are invested when they are allowed to put their good ideas in place themselves and the whole organization benefits from their commitment.

A company can give employees permission to put their ideas into action but there will be little change if there isn't a process that enables them to make it happen. When I work with organizations I train them in the creative problem-solving process. This step-by-step process gives people a way to take an idea and move it through to implementation. It gives workers a common language and a consistent approach to problem solving—a forum to pull their minds together. Sometimes these sessions have the feeling of classic "brain storming." The difference is that this process takes the ideas and moves them all the way to an action plan. Creative problem solving provides a way to apply creativity.

Wright

It sounds like creative problem solving is a valuable tool for business. Tell me more about this process.

Prince

In the late 1930s Alex Osborne (the "O" in BBDO Advertising) was challenged to come up with a process to enable people in the advertising business to deliver creativity at a consistent level to their clients. His efforts led to the development of "brainstorming" (which is a term Alex Osborne himself coined). In 1950 he teamed up with Professor Sid Parnes and went on to create what is known today as the Osborne-Parnes Model of Creative Problem Solving. This process has been proven over the years to be a consistent way to find new solutions in every industry where it has been applied.

Creative problem solving has been fine-tuned and adapted over time as proponents have applied creativity to the process itself. I now utilize a simpler version of creative problem solving that has only four steps with the principles of creative thinking applied in each one.

Before we take a look at the process let me pause here to say that creative problem solving is just as valuable when done at an individual level. I keep a flip chart at the ready in my home so that when faced with family or individual challenges I can go through the process and come up with a personal action plan. But today I'd like to talk about using the process with a group.

Typically, when you walk into a creative problem-solving session you bring a challenge or a problem to work on. Someone writes the problem on a flip chart or blackboard where everyone can see it and then you move into the first step, which is *fact-finding.*

In fact-finding, the group begins to look at what they know or think they know about the problem. They also begin to explore what they don't know about the problem, what things have been tried in the past that didn't work, and why they didn't work. The more they can know about a challenge the clearer the actual problem will become. Jumping straight into ideas without the illumination that fact-finding provides is like jumping into a muddy river.

The second step is *challenge clarification.* Oftentimes after fact finding is done, a group discovers that they are working on a symptom of the problem instead of the problem itself. Sometimes they find that the problem needs to be broken down into smaller pieces—pieces that can be tackled successfully one by one. In this step the problem is redefined.

The third step is *idea generation*. This is a high-energy step and the one that more people are familiar with. Out of all the steps this one is the closest to a classical brainstorming session. It is the place where the group comes up with a long list of solutions to the now redefined problem.

The last step is *action planning*. In this step the group creates an action plan with specific tasks, dates for the tasks to be completed, and people's names assigned to each task. This is the place where the ideas are moved into implementation and where creative solutions are applied.

Key to this whole process is the use of the principles of creative thinking that I talked about earlier. The principle of separating divergent and convergent thinking is used in every single step. For example, in the fact-finding step a long list of facts about the problem is created. For this to work, the group has to set aside evaluation of each fact until the whole list is created. Judgment of the value of each fact is held until the group decides to move into converging. Then at a set time, or when the list feels complete, the group will begin to converge, narrowing the list down to the most important, applicable facts. This process is repeated when the group again creates a list of challenge statements then later converges or narrows those down to the ones that best redefine the problem. Then again, in the idea-generating step, the group holds off evaluation of ideas until a list is created. The list of ideas is then narrowed to the best ideas. This happens again in the action-planning step. The principles of diverging then converging are used in every step of the process.

Creative problem solving is a way to apply the principles of creative thinking (diverging then converging) to specific challenges. In business it can become an established way to put creative ideas into action.

Wright

How would an organization use creative problem solving in sales for example?

Prince

Good question. Many organizations have applied creative problem solving to things like new product development. The truth is, however, creative problem solving can be applied at any place within an organization.

Selling is one of the most powerful places where an organization can utilize the creative problem-solving Process. Customers want creative solutions to their needs. Clients expect a salesperson to come in, describe their product then leave. Imagine instead a salesperson who comes in, takes the time to do enough good fact-findings to really understand the client's challenge, and then comes back with a practical solution. This is customer-focused selling at its best. Wouldn't it be nice to be invited into a client's office for a pow-wow rather than allowed a few minutes for a pitch? No doubt about it, when a salesperson is a good problem-solver he or she stands out from the competition.

Wright

So, salespeople need creative problem-solving skills.

Prince

Absolutely. Creative problem solving in sales can be a powerful way of driving top line revenues. Another advantage of using this process with people who work in sales is that it can provide a way for typically independent salespeople to work together. It provides a forum where they can share ideas, learn from each other, then go out and use these ideas to sell in different markets or to different customer groups.

Sharing success stories with each other at these creative problem-solving (CPS) sessions provides the opportunity for salespeople to pick up on each other's successes and then go back and implement them for themselves.

Wright

I can see where being in a CPS session and hearing about others' successes can be a strong motivator to making changes back in the home territory.

Prince

Absolutely. By trading on other's experience I don't have to reinvent the wheel. I can simply take their tried solutions and reapply them.

Wright

What else does an idea factory need to be successful?

Prince

Once people have developed strong problem solving skills, there needs to be a way to coordinate efforts to drive solutions within the organization. At this point I believe what is needed is a method to develop a visionary and practical strategic plan. Most business leaders learn strategic planning from the budgeting process. But the budgeting process requires looking backward. The question is always, how did we do? We look at the numbers, decide how much we need to gain in the upcoming year, put in a little wiggle room and *voilà!* we have a strategic plan. It is a backward-facing process for driving business forward.

What businesses really need is a full and focused strategic planning process—a process where they first look forward to future goals, take time to stop and compare those goals to their current situation, then figure out a plan that will move them to where they want to be.

This shifting the perspective forward opens an organization up to new possibilities. It can be the very thing that "unsticks" it, enabling it to truly become an idea factory. Instead of being stifled by what is, employees can be excited and motivated by what *can* be.

Top-level management knows they must have a strategy to move their business forward. Only the most successful business professionals understand that to make real progress, strategic planning needs to happen at all levels. In these organizations each employee develops his or her own individual strategic plan. This plan relates directly to their particular job situations as well as the organization's goals. These individual plans then roll up into one over-all organizational strategy. This gives the business a consistent focus from front line to top line.

A one hundred-watt light bulb can be seen from a distance of about one mile. A ten-watt laser light can be seen from the moon. The difference is focused energy. Strategic plans focus the energy of an entire organization on achieving a well-defined desired future state.

Wright

What is required of senior management to maintain a truly innovative organization?

Prince

The executives I work with often talk about staying ahead of the competition. They recognize that to stay ahead they have to be willing to make changes, but fear of failure often makes them unwilling to take the risks that are inherent in change. By systematically looking ahead an organization can gather data points about their future. Often these data points will reveal a pattern. These patterns help in recognizing areas of predictability in their businesses.

Finding a measure of predictability will minimize the fear of risk and maximize and an organization's confidence. These patterns can also be indicators of future challenges enabling a business to change its strategy before problems occur. Developing the skill to look forward to future goals rather than back at past failures is key.

Wright

Okay, I'm sold. If I'm in senior management, how do I make this happen in my business?

Prince

The principles of creative thinking, creative problem solving, and forward-looking strategy are all skills that can be learned. The problem with most training is that it teaches concepts not skills. For true skill building to happen, individuals have to go through a learning experience then have an opportunity to take what they learned and practice it in the real world.

An example might be learning to swim. You can go to a classroom and watch a video of someone swimming. You can discuss thoroughly all the strokes, how to breathe, and how to get in and out of the water; but you will never really learn to swim unless you jump in. And even after you are in the water, to become a better swimmer you need good coaching and regular practice. If you achieve some level of success—let's say you are able to make it all the way across the pool—it is likely that you will be willing to jump in again. Experiencing small successes reinforces your desire to practice and to build your skills, which enables you to be even more successful, which increases your desire to learn and practice.

Instead of forcing training on employees, truly innovative organizations find ways to create this kind of positively reinforcing skill-building loop. They do this by providing people ways to practice, making skilled coaches available, and giving them constructive feedback so that their desire to learn is continually increased.

Wright

So, innovative strategies are key to the success and survival of the business of the future. How do organizations start this process so they can be prepared?

Prince

The first place to start is a company's belief system. Every organization and each individual in that organization carry beliefs that affect every decision they make. The belief that employees have the capacity to be innovative in their jobs is fundamental in a true idea factory.

Many people tell me that it is hard to change. It isn't hard to change your behavior if you first change your beliefs. For leaders in an organization to say that they are going to become more creative and innovative is one thing, for this to actually happen, management has to believe that taking the time to implement new ideas will benefit the company.

The leadership of a company has to believe that supporting their people in the implementation of new ideas will grow the bottom line. Whether they use creative problem solving or another methodology, successful businesses encourage their people to innovate in their jobs. The creativity of the individuals in the company is truly the company's greatest resource, and its best chance of making it in the future.

If you look at the overall cost of running an organization, the most significant investment a company makes is in its people. The only way to adequately utilize that investment is to tap into the creativity that each person brings to the company. This creativity can spark the innovation that will keep an organization ahead of the competition. Employees are willing to go the extra mile when they believe that their ideas are valued.

Once idea implementation brings successes these need to be captured and shared with others in the organization. This can happen when employees are allowed to interact with and learn more about the other departments or divisions of the company. Seeing the successful implementation of new ideas across a wide range of jobs reinforces the belief that workers are a part of an innovative, creative organization—an idea factory.

The last piece of putting all this together is developing a strong strategic plan for the idea factory. The strategic plan is the roadmap to success. It is one thing to say that we are going to change; it's another to say that we are planning for the continued change that will move us toward our vision of a successful future.

Wright

Frank, I really appreciate your taking the time to answer my questions. I feel I have a much better understanding of what being creative really means, in business and in our individual lives. I have learned a lot today. I'm sure our readers have too.

Prince

Thank you for the opportunity.

Wright

Today we've been talking with Frank Prince. Frank takes a no nonsense approach to implementing innovation within organizations. Since 1988 he has focused his work on delivering skills such as leadership, creativity, and strategic planning to individuals within organizations. These skills have proven again and again to drive top line sales and bottom line results.

How does he do it? He says by tapping into the most underused resource that exists in business today—the minds of people. Frank works at all levels in organizations. He gives upfront salespeople creative problem-solving skills that can be used to institute a customer oriented sales force. He works with middle management to evolve their skills from "manager-ship" to leadership skills. He also facilitates strategic planning sessions that enable them to put new ideas into action. He works with senior executives designing and developing the "idea factories" that drive the innovation and positive change that will insure their success in the future.

Frank, thanks for being with us today on *Blueprint for Success.*

About Frank Prince...

FRANK PRINCE is President and Founder of Unleash Your Mind Consulting and author of over thirty books and articles in the field of creativity and innovation in business. His clients include several Fortune 100 firms including Time Inc., Procter & Gamble, Perrier, PepsiCo, and Nabisco. Frank is a frequent keynote speaker around the world focusing on "creating 'idea factories' " within organizations. He has delivered keynotes at conferences in South Africa, Turkey, Japan, and throughout the United States and Europe.

Frank A. Prince

Unleash Your Mind

512 McClurg Court, Suite # 4807

Chicago, IL 60611

312.828.9245

frankprince@mindspring.com

www.frankprince.com

www.unleashyourmind.com

www.speedsleep.com

www.thoughtfreegolf.com

Chapter Four

An *interview with…*

Suzanne Evans

David Wright (Wright)

Today we're talking with Suzanne Evans. She is an action expert. When individuals and businesses are looking for a blueprint for success they seek her coaching, sharp instincts, and accountability. After working for the nation's largest union, being a professional actress, a nationally ranked water skier, a high school teacher, and an assistant producer to five Broadway shows (all before the age of thirty), Suzanne began using her life experiences to coach a wide range of people on living their fullest potential. She created a private coaching practice with over forty clients in one year and launched three businesses in a four-month timeframe. Action comes naturally.

Suzanne received her bachelor's degree from Lees-McRae College, her master's from New York University, and is a graduate of Coach U. She is a sought-after speaker, workshop facilitator, and coach. Her coaching has been described as tough, honest, keen, and caring. She is a member of the International Coaching Federation and has coached hundreds of clients to take action and seek change. She is the owner of www.blueprintlifecoaching.com, www.thevablueprint.com, and www.coachaccelerationsystem.com.

She resides in Maplewood, New Jersey. When she is not coaching, she is tracking with her Westie, Lucky Boy, going to a favorite restaurant, watching college basketball, or traveling.

Suzanne, I know you believe that one of the most important elements of the success formula is action. Why is that?

Suzanne Evans (Evans)

Actually, I believe it to be the single most important factor in having any level of success. Certainly, it is the motor that moves success. By definition, "action" is the state or process of doing. It seems fairly simple. To do is to act, and if you are not in a state of motion it is impossible to move toward your goals. Newton's Law states, "Every object in the state of uniform motion tends to stay in that state of motion unless an external force is applied to it." So, the universe has already established that once we begin "doing" it will automatically support that process to continue. Action creates more action. Ideas, hopes, and plans are meaningless unless implemented.

So many people stay in learning mode; they collect information, focus on weighing decisions and forget to take action. When I am working with clients I quite often see that they have enough information and education. They do not need to wait any longer—they just need to leap. So without action, success is impossible.

There is also the try trap. A client will say, "I am trying to get going," or, "I am trying to put it all together." Take a moment to analyze "try." Everyone reading, right now: try to put this book on your lap. What happened? You either did it or you didn't. There is no "try" in action—you simply do. A great place to start action is to eliminate trying. Every time you find yourself wanting to "try" something, change the word to "do" and just go. Before you know it, you will be headed toward success.

Wright

So, you mentioned the dictionary definition of action, but what is your personal definition?

Evans

My personal definition is: "facing forward with possibility." Action is relative to the individual and to the circumstance. I wouldn't dare say the definition is moving forward because often successful action can be standing still, stepping back, or waiting. So, action doesn't always mean movement, but the idea is that whether you are moving or waiting, you are always facing forward toward your success. Benjamin Franklin said, "Never confuse motion with action."

A common place to get stuck is in your circumstances. It is easy to confuse circumstances with possibility. Circumstances are things that have happened to you . . . possibility is your capability and passion.

My definition of facing forward with possibility is a way to remind yourself of what is possible for you.

Wright

How do you face forward? How do you become a "doer"?

Evans

There are a few easy and practical ways to get unstuck and get moving:

1. Create an accomplishments list. Forget about what you are trying to do and focus on what you have done. What are you most proud of doing? What have you done already today? Those accomplishments don't have to be worthy of a Nobel Peace Prize. I am talking about simple accomplishments such as cleaning out the garage or playing the turkey in the third grade play. Think of what those accomplishments are, no matter how small, and write them down.

2. Stop reading and start doing. Get away from being a self-help junkie. Don't get me wrong, I love self-help books and motivational materials, but they can actually keep you stuck. If you find yourself with a shelf full of books and a list of goals a mile long with nothing checked off, then change your approach.

3. Operate from where you want to be. Start living your life as if you have already reached your goals and design your activities from that mindset. It is an automatic trigger for action and keeps you motivated around what you want to accomplish.

4. Ask, look for, and create accountability. If you know you struggle with keeping the keeping-on going, then set yourself up for success with a coach, a friend, or a system. This is why coaching is so integral to people's success.

Sometimes all it takes is a consistent reminder of what your goals are and you are on your way to achieving them.

Wright

Speaking of a consistent reminder, once you have started some of these processes, how do you keep the momentum going?

Evans

That is a very important point because action in spurts is not as effective as long-term consistent action and that takes momentum. If you watch any athletic event then you can see that it takes skill, stamina, and endurance. However, it is the momentum formula that sinks the basket just before the buzzer or gives the runner that jolt of energy to speed across the finish line first. Momentum is key.

One way to create momentum is to keep increasing your goals and improving yourself. If you reach the finish line, then find the next race. If you launch the business, then start creating the next. Goals are the gifts that keep on giving. In each new one there is more possibility, more opportunity, and more joy. Another way to ensure momentum is to only do what you are best at and delegate the rest. It is an energy drain and a demotivator to get wrapped up trying to do it all and be it all.

I personally believe that virtual assistants are going to change the face of the solopreneur, entrepreneur, and small business world. Delegating and outsourcing work you do not enjoy or excel in is the key opportunity to being able to work at your highest capability. I simply couldn't do what I truly enjoy if it weren't for working with virtual assistants. They are an ideal example of how to create momentum and delegate.

Finally, you have to set boundaries and determine what you are and are not willing to do or take on. Having clear boundaries allows you to continue on a long-term action path free of the external force or interruption that Newton talks about.

Wright

Suzanne, how do you personally apply these principles every day in your life? How do you stay in action?

Evans

Well, I am very fortunate. I had incredible examples of action from a very young age with my parents. They were always "doers" and they taught me the importance of being motivated, showing up in your own life, and creating your own change. One of my greatest lessons was watching them always move on. No matter what the circumstances or the outcomes to any situation, they would keep going, which was an extremely valuable example and model to emulate. On the other hand, I can certainly relate to feeling stuck and overwhelmed, so I always make certain to surround myself with people who are action-oriented and who help motivate me and keep my momentum going. Whether it is a coach, business partner, colleagues, or friends, those you surround yourself with are ultimately the people you become. Be sure to choose action-oriented people in your life.

I also make it my goal to do a little each day with whatever projects I am working on at the time. This is not for the sake of keeping myself busy, but doing more of what I enjoy, what I am excited about, or passionate about. I make a conscious effort to make time for planning, building, and living the business and life goals I have. It is as simple as clearing the decks on occasion. If you really want to make it happen, clear the decks and make it happen.

I also use a careful lens when I am viewing my goals and my action steps. Deciding to climb a mountain seems like a huge undertaking if you continually count the paces and focus on how much farther you have to go; but if you keep focused on the summit and why you are going there in the first place, then the dream seems sweeter and the action simpler. Be certain to have clarity around your goals because there is no quicker way to stop dead in your tracks than to be in the middle of doing, creating, and taking action and have no idea what your purpose is. Clarity is important in order for anyone to stay in action.

I also avoid what I call "poverty" or "scarcity mentality" because it can be extremely exhausting. Scarcity mentality says: I feel like I will never get enough done, I will never finish, I will never have enough, and things are so hard. Flipping that idea and knowing that I have enough time and I have done enough eliminates the constant pressure to perform.

Wright

Why are so many people afraid to take action? What stops them?

Evans

Fear and confusion. If you are in action, then you are in queue for success and that just scares the hell out of most people. Change is exhilarating and frightening.

Mark Twain said, "Twenty years from now you will be more disappointed by the things you didn't do than by the ones you did. So throw off the bowlines. Sail away from the safe harbor. Catch the trade winds in your sails. Explore. Dream. Discover."

As fearful as taking action can be, not taking action is one of the regrets I most often see. Fear is a thorn in the side of action. We have all been there. We start to make a move toward our goal and a voice pops up reminding us of the possibility of failure, and fear kicks in. Fear has two purposes that it consistently serves: to protect us and to paralyze us. If you go for a walk and come upon a snake coiled and ready to strike, your "protection" fear would most likely kick in and encourage you to walk away, remove yourself from the situation, and flee. Now, if because of this frightening situation that you encountered on your walk you decide to never go for a walk again, then fear has paralyzed you. Spend some time knowing the difference, understanding the flow of one to another, and how you can use fear as motivation.

Another "stop sign" I see for action is distraction. I like to call it "Bright Shiny Object Syndrome." Just as we start our rhythm of momentum moving toward our goals, we allow ourselves to be distracted by the next best thing.

I was recently coaching Julie, a client with great passion and a sharp wit. She put great time, excitement, and effort into fulfilling her lifelong dream of starting a mediation business. Out of the blue, I got an e-mail from her asking what I thought about another business venture. Curious, but not surprised, I e-mailed and asked how this new idea aligned with her vision for her mediation business. Her response was simple: "I get it."

The bright shiny object stopped her flow of action. You know the saying, "the grass is always greener on the other side." We just can't stop looking and grabbing at the "what if" flying by. Train yourself to let things go. Not every idea needs energy and not every thought demands attention. Are you interested in a new idea because it is appealing and exciting or do you need a break from what you are currently working toward? Continually remind yourself of what you really want, why you want it, and how you are working toward that. Don't constantly stand poised and ready to catch the next best thing.

Wright

Several times you have mentioned doing nothing as action. How does that work?

Evans

People can fall into action overload. They are running, going, doing, but ultimately getting nothing accomplished. Action can be mistaken for performing or doing. You don't have to solve every problem, meet every need, and make yourself feel "busy." Analyze what needs to happen and what needs to be ignored.

Doing the same thing over and over and expecting a different result is the definition of insanity. Sometimes it's better to step out of action so you can analyze and determine what your next step will be. Why have an argument with reality? Action is not about doing without purpose or process. Having a vision, having a plan, and being clear about your next step will enable your action to lead to success.

I also use a "Tolerations List." This is a good way to find out what is taking up space in my life. Anything that is going on in my life is going to be taking up space. If I am tolerating too many things, where is the room to take action to go forward with my goals? Humans have learned how to tolerate a lot! They put up with, accept, take on, and are dragged down by other people's behavior, situations, and unmet needs. They accept crossed boundaries, incompletion, frustrations, problems, and even their own behavior. They tolerate a lot more than they think.

I ask my clients, "What are you tolerating?" and ask them to spend some time making a list of those items. The goal is to eliminate those items and have a toleration-free life; but this does not happen overnight. Sometimes just becoming aware of and articulating these tolerations will bring them to the forefront of the soul and the client will naturally start handling, eliminating, fixing, weeding through, and resolving these tolerations.

Wright

What is the largest misconception about action?

Evans

It's that there is a magic formula, a magic pill, something that will make everything okay and make all your actions kick into gear. I often hear things such as, "When I pay off my credit card bills—" or "When I leave my spouse—" or "When the kids go to school, leave school, leave home—" or "When I lose weight—" I have heard them all. There is no right time. There is only now and waiting for the right time will get you exactly there—waiting. There is no moment when all the stars align and the moon shifts and you get what you want. Chunks of action steps each and every day are key to success. And when someone tells you that you should do something, keep in mind that it is always someone else's good idea. It has very little to do with you.

I also hear clients discuss "wishing" quite a bit. They often say, "I wish I could go to school, I wish I could change jobs, I wish, I wish, I wish." Every time you have a wish, switch it to action. Wishing can be fun and while it can open you up to ideas and creativity, how can you couple it with action? Ask yourself what you can do today and in this moment to move toward your wish. Wishing is great for stars and chicken bones, but it doesn't get you out of where you are and into where you want to be.

One of my favorite African proverbs says: "When you pray, move your feet." What are you wishing or praying for and how can you stand up and take action toward it today?

Wright

That brings up an interesting question about the Law of Attraction. There is a lot of discussion around that topic lately. How do your thoughts on action relate to the Law of Attraction?

Evans

The Law of Attraction serves a wonderful purpose for mindset, clarity, and visioning. You must have the action piece in it or it becomes worthless. You can have a clear idea of what you want and focus on attracting that, but it will take steps and movement toward that goal every day. You can sit at home all day long and repeat what you want to achieve in your life, but if you put no action behind it then you will certainly still be sitting at home waiting for something to happen. Think in terms of these simple steps when you are using the Law of Attraction:

Concretize the idea or desire.
Create a clear vision around your idea or desire.
Believe that you can achieve it.
Design a daily action plan to get there.

Wright

How did you use these steps and other action steps to create a successful coaching and speaking business? What did your action journey look like?

Evans

It really happened in a seven-step process, although I didn't know that at that time.

First, I acknowledged that I wanted more for my life than I currently had. I agreed to give up white-knuckling events both personally and professionally. I didn't have to know what every move would be, to have all the answers, or to know all the steps in the plan. I just needed to get a plan together.

I remember clearly the day I agreed to embrace uncertainty. I had a high school friend who had died from cancer at age twenty-nine and I thought to myself that uncertainty is present whether I control it or not. A great many things in life were out of my control, so I needed to start controlling the things I could. I also decided I would show up in my life every day and work toward what I wanted. For the most part I was happy, well paid, and "together," but I woke up every day with a nagging thought that said "show up in your life, find a passion path, and stop living small." It scared me to death, but I agreed to listen and deal with the uncertainty that might come.

Second, I decided that if I was going to embrace uncertainty I was going to need some help doing it, so I began to assemble a team. I made it my job to build a team around me for accountability, for support, to be a sounding board, and give me a kick in the pants. I hired a coach, started a coaching program, joined communities, and found mentors who would hold me accountable for what I wanted to accomplish. They also supported me in dealing with fear and uncertainty.

Third, every day I worked at it on some level. No matter how large or small, I took a stride toward building my coaching business. I revisited and reevaluated my goals daily. I always wanted the goal more than anybody else did. I made sure I was the loudest cheerleader, the most aggressive linebacker, and the head coach in my own process.

My team was there to help, but not to do the work. I worked on my personal and my professional life so that I could build a business from abundance and not scarcity. And I made certain to have the financial and emotional reserves needed so I was able to focus on the goal and to stay in action mode.

Fourth, I believed my goal was achieved before I even started. Was it ego? Maybe. Confidence? Yes. Decisiveness. Absolutely!

I began to understand that decisiveness was one of the most important components to success. I researched successful leaders and found that a common thread in their success was being clear and decisive and then going into immediate action. The best way to illustrate this is a simple logic puzzle:

Five monkeys are sitting on a limb. Two decide to jump off. How many are left on the limb?

Five.

Deciding is not doing. It is essential, but once the decision is made you have to move straight into action.

I stopped wasting time weighing an overwhelming number of options and went with my gut. Was I 100 percent right on everything? Nope. But I saved tons of time and I made the right move 90 percent of the time. Those are good enough stats for me.

I also eliminated the doubting thoughts. I knew those thoughts were not helping me to be decisive so I eliminated them. That also meant I eliminated people who were naysayers. I didn't spend time or energy trying to convince people that I would succeed. I just kept plugging away. Action speaks louder than words. I also learned to change the subject very well. If someone had something negative to say I would volley it back and ask him or her to turn the complaint into a request. Amazing how that silences people.

Fifth, I learned to say no. It is a complete sentence that requires no beginning, no middle, and no end. Saying no always shocks people, but it is powerful and much like a muscle—the more you use it the stronger it is. The less you use it the more painful it is. I began asking: "Does _____ move me forward to my goal? Does this bring me joy? Is this a necessity?" If the answer was, "No," it was eliminated.

I also made time for the goals and for the action. If you are already feeling like you don't have enough time, then you must clear the decks. You must make space for what you want. It may mean burning some bridges, but go ahead and strike the match.

Sixth, I continually asked:

- for support
- for guidance
- for mentoring
- for help
- for resources
- for a push
- for a hand
- for anything I needed when I needed it.

You need to get comfortable with asking for support. You are one person taking action toward success, but if you had others working for you and with you, imagine where you could go.

And seventh, I did and continue to do a lot of celebrating. I celebrate the big things, the small things. I found what brought me great joy is celebration, so I chose to use it as a reward, motivation, or relaxation. What is the point in any success if you don't take the time to enjoy it? Just as you have to choose action, you must choose joy. It is a decision.

What works for you? For me it is traveling, restaurants, training my Westie (or him training me), and spending time with my family. Start making your own list.

Wright

Suzanne, hearing what your process was, if you could leave the readers with one singular insight, what would it be?

Evans

It would be that success and action don't start with someone else or something else. You can never look externally for something that you have to do. It's that simple. I could spend a few minutes talking about why, but the why isn't important. You have to do the work.

So, I would tell the readers to put down the book (my apologies to the next chapter) and do something right now to head toward success.

Make a call, make a list, set a date, write an accomplishments list, write a thank-you note, quit your job, start a job, apologize to someone, open a savings account, open your bills, throw out the junk food, hire a coach, find an online community, clean your desk drawer, call your mom, listen to an inspiring piece of music, write a piece of music, share your wealth, share your knowledge. Stand up right where you are and do something. The success is not in the size of the action, it is in the commitment. So you might as well start now. There will never be a better time.

About Suzanne Evans...

SUZANNE EVANS is the Blueprint Coach. As a coach, speaker, and trainer, she works with individuals and groups to create success by design. She is best known for taking people from idea to action through her powerful coaching. She is the owner of three coaching businesses and works with a variety of people from different backgrounds.

Suzanne Evans
Blueprint Coaching
Maplewood, NJ
917.385.1385
Suzanne@blueprintlifecoaching.com
www.blueprintlifecoaching.com
www.thevablueprint.com
www.coachaccelerationsystem.com

Chapter **Five**

An *interview with...*

Dr. J. Gregory Gillum, CPCC

David Wright (Wright)

Today we're talking with Dr. J. Gregory Gillum. A Kentucky native, Dr. Gillum is a keynote speaker, author and acclaimed entrepreneur business coach. Dr. Gillum also serves as the Chief Executive Officer of the humanfusion group of companies. As the lead executive coach and trainer, he specializes in leadership development applications, business performance coaching, emotional intelligence, and guiding transformational change in individuals and organizations. A frequent keynote speaker in the areas of human performance and potential, Dr. Gillum spent six years on the faculty of the Medical College of Virginia, and eight years in marketing and senior management with GlaxoSmithKline. He earned his doctorate from the University of Kentucky and his professional coaching credentials from the Coaches Training Institute in San Rafael, California. He lives with his wife and two children on a farm in central Kentucky.

Greg, welcome to *Blueprint for Success*.

Wright

This book is about blueprints. What is your personal blueprint for success?

Greg Gillum (Gillum)

There are clearly many factors that contribute to one's success in life, but my personal blueprint for success consistently revolves around my spiritual center. In parallel, my mental blueprint is dominated by connecting what I am doing in the moment to my larger purpose and mission. Living on purpose and operating with a mission are both spiritual pursuits. Just like any great corporation needs a clearly defined purpose and mission to drive decision-making and performance throughout the organization, so do individuals. Below is my personal statement of purpose:

I breathe . . .
to fulfill God's purpose in my life,
relentlessly exploring my potential
that honors the
Spirit
that resides in me.

Notice how "potential" is incorporated into my statement of purpose, and that the chief means by which I fulfill my purpose is through relentless exploration. Warren Bennis speaks of professional reinvention as a necessary tool for future leadership. What he means is that we must explore many pathways if we are to truly discover what our potential holds. Personally I have shifted directions in my career about every three to five years since 1990. This exploration is not for everyone, but for those who have the mental and physical discipline required to be successful during these transitions, it can open up the world of possibility.

And possibility begins with awareness. I can generate an unusual amount of physical energy when I work with clients through the progression from unawareness to awareness. I simply love to learn, and I am continually drawn to the process of learning. My ideal vacation would be traveling to some unknown land or engaging in some experience that allows me to learn something new. I am a student of the Italian Renaissance, so exploring Florence, the birthplace of the Renaissance, is undeniably one of the greatest thrills in my life. All that said, it's important to note, however, that the outcome of the learning is less significant than the process of exploring.

In addition, my personal mission incorporates many aspects of my personality and interests (e.g., coaching, teaching, being creative, exploring internal motivation, understanding innovation, etc.) into the driving force that fuels my ambition in life more than anything—introducing another human being to a concept that he or she may have never considered, a concept that has the potential to completely change a person's life. Below is my personal statement of mission:

I engage . . .
those who are willing
to walk into new rooms,
seeking windows
never opened.

When you hear about "alignment thinking" or "alignment leadership," this is the process they are referring to. Your mission is your tactical plan. Your purpose is your strategic plan. Your mission should support your purpose and every action you take should support both. Therefore, my mission of helping others see through new windows is the tactical plan that fuels my daily journey of purpose and potential.

Since my spiritual core is unshakably rooted in Christian values, my point of view is influenced by my relationship with Christ and what He represented—His mission was to serve, not to be served—and I prayerfully engage in servant leadership every day with those I work with, whether that person is a client or a colleague.

I can get totally absorbed in a process. I can get into a mental zone that psychologist Mihaly Csikszentmihalyi called flow. I lose track of time when I am helping someone see something from a different perspective, which is the chief reason I enjoy coaching so much.

Servant leadership is based on recognizing a need, then meeting it, and in leadership circles we call this skill empathy. The skill of empathy has been recently well examined as a competency in the development of emotional intelligence (i.e., Emotional Quotient—EQ) and leadership, and how leaders understand the basics of social awareness in serving others. We understand the people and the world around us a little better each time we can help other people meet their needs. We look into a better reflection of our soul when we allow empathy to embrace our heart and mind first, and then use it to enrich the life of someone else.

Having also spent considerable time with the process of understanding my values, it makes the process of decision-making clearer if what I am doing or being asked to do supports and reflects my purpose and mission, and if it also utilizes my personal values, I know I am walking on the right path. If not, I choose proactively not to get involved. Since discovering and utilizing this method around decision-making several years ago, I can say "no" to the wrong things and "yes" to the right things.

A tacit knowledge of your values, along with a keen sense of your mission and purpose, allow you to be very efficient in making better decisions in the present—in the now. And this process provides the strategic map that allows you to see if you are riding on the right bus, sitting in the right seat, and always driving in the right direction.

Wright

Human potential is an interesting area of study. Why are you so passionate about the subject?

Gillum

I guess I am so passionate about human potential because it's the one innate thing we all have in common as human beings. Human potential is the original strategic plan. All of us are created for a reason; we are each given a master plan to write in the limited time we have on this planet. And on this journey we have an awesome responsibility to explore our potential, not just for our own good and the good of those we influence during our lifetime, but for the good of society at large.

In Joseph Campbell's work on the epic journey of the hero, the last responsibility after finishing the course, after completing the heroic chapter, is to teach the village everything they had learned along the way. Thus knowledge gained on our journey is not simply for us, but more importantly for everyone else. If I neglect my potential, I not only cheat myself, but I cheat you as well. Likewise, we are all endowed with specific gifts and talents, but they aren't exclusively for us to use personally, they are for the other people in our life. Think about it: An author's gift can only be experienced by the reader. An actor's gift is only experienced by a theatergoer. A coach's gift is only experienced by the player. This responsibility to give back creates the basis of leadership and weaves the underlying fabric of social capital. Becoming a hero is a privilege, and that privilege is met with a challenge of a greater responsibility—the responsibility of positive change and social influence that forms the underpinning of human potential.

Wright

If you could condense your personal success down to a "single most important ingredient," what would you like people to learn from your own path to human potential?

Gillum

It may be too simplistic to distill success down to a single ingredient. Let's face it—personal growth and development is very hard work, and is certainly not intended for those not willing to make the necessary sacrifices to achieve it. The road less taken is walked by only a few because success is bred on the road marked by the most resistance, not the least. When success happens fast or too easy, it usually has a short life span.

The path of least resistance is more congested because not as much is required of us, and in a world that makes many demands, the easier path can emerge as a brilliant disguise, masking as the freeway we should all be traveling on. If everyone else is on the road, and if everyone is heading in the same direction, we must be doing something right, wouldn't you think? Well, most likely not, and all the while the obscure, steep little mountain pass that will eventually lead us to personal success and fulfillment is going in the opposite direction, so it gets ignored or suppressed. Going against the grain is never in vogue because it has never been nor will it ever be the easy road to take. It takes a lot of fortitude to venture over into the oncoming traffic, but the risk of not doing so is worth paying attention to—nothing ventured always leads to nothing gained.

All that being said, meaningful human achievement against the natural resistance inherent with success requires a substantial expenditure of energy. It's the manner in which we control and manage that energy that leads to the unveiling of the true secret that unlocks personal growth and development.

The most efficient way I have found to manage energy is by planning and acting, thinking and executing within the boundaries of a system. My personal success relies on my conformity to the success system I have developed over the years. And believe me, as a non-conformist, this isn't easy for me. For myself, and for those clients willing to examine their potential through the humanfusion coaching practice, we label the success system "the discipline of potential." The system is designed to maximize efficiencies while allowing significant flexibility and creativity. I manage my time, my daily priorities, and my personal and professional business all within the context of a system. This way, if I monitor my system closely enough—paying attention to what is working well and what isn't—it makes the task of refining and improving the system much easier. If something isn't working well I can spend a little time correcting the issue, and then begin to monitor the change. The process is very similar to the Japanese concept of kaizen, or continuous improvement, where subtle changes in the system will have a dramatic effect on the outcome. The very idea is embedded in the circular logo of humanfusion, forming the core identity of our corporate branding.

The most important thing to understand is that the system of success that I have in place today in no way resembles the system I had in place when I began my personal journey over fifteen years ago. That is not to say, however, that all of my original ideas for my system weren't useful; it's just that development evolves over time, and what I am doing now may not be what I am doing this time next year. One needs to be creative and flexible when dealing with dynamic processes. When a baby becomes a toddler, his or her needs change. As you grow in your potential and progress through new stages in your development, your needs will change as well. A close, honest, and introspective look at the fine-tuning of your system is what drives success and what sets the stage for exploring your potential.

Wright

Can you define human potential and what it means to be human?

Gillum

A simple way to view the progression of human potential is through the continual pursuit of growth and development in the four domains that constitute life: physical, mental, social-emotional, and spiritual. Easier said than done, of course, but nonetheless, if you have a plan in each area, and are working on developing disciplines in each area, on some level you are in pursuit of your potential. And please note that the emphasis here is focused on pursuit, not on attainment.

The question of what it is to be human is very complex, and one that obviously needs more attention and treatment than we can give here, but I think it is important to consider the basics of being human, what distinguishing characteristics we possess, and what we can become if we accept the challenge that the pursuit of human potential offers us.

What sets us apart from our animal friends is our highly developed brain, with the inherent capability of thinking both in pragmatic and visionary ways. We have the capacity to reason. We possess the ability to analyze our motives. Humans are particularly adept at utilizing systems of communication for self-expression, the exchange of ideas, and organizing disparate information. This latter, synthesizing aspect of the human mind is emerging as being very important in the information age we now live in, and undoubtedly will be important well into the future.

As it relates to potential, we humans are noted for the desire to understand and influence the world around us. These natural curiosities have led to continual human development and societal progression—think about the Renaissance. That period represented a quantum leap from the status quo of the Dark Ages—it was completely fueled by humans who were insanely curious about how things worked and how those things could be improved. These types of innovations spur humanity in the direction and evolution of potential.

Furthermore, the human ability to think abstractly is unparalleled in the animal kingdom. Humans possess consciousness, self-awareness, independent will, and a mind that can arrange information that comprises the mental process of thinking with a purpose in mind and a subsequent action that can be realized. Humans are unique in our ability to effect an action that was previously only something imagined. So creative imagination and independent will make up the one-two punch that allows us to think and animate actions that promote our development. All of these characteristics make us uniquely endowed to pursue our innate ability to develop ourselves into the beings we are meant to be—whatever potential the world has in store for us.

What we can become if we accept the challenge of pursuing our potential is a driving force of positive change in the world. I say that because not all agents of change will have positive intentions. But assuming our motives are pure and trustworthy, the pursuit of potential can offer someone a real chance at becoming noteworthy—someone who will impact the world in a significant, meaningful way.

Wright

You work with clients who likely ask, "What am I supposed to be doing with my life?" Hopefully that question has entered our minds from time to time. Is finding the meaning of life an important task to undertake?

Gillum

It may be the most important question we ever ask ourselves. If someone is wrestling with that question on some level, he or she is at least searching for and looking at the right map, seeking the right direction for his or her life. People who ask that question of themselves have at least some conscious desire to examine their own potential.

The question, or at least a variant of that question, is a fairly common one that emerges during the coaching process with every client. The issue surrounding life's meaning is natural to consider, especially for those who are engaged in performance coaching. Clients, to some degree, are looking for ways to catalyze their growth and enhance their functioning in a certain capacity.

The answer to "meaning" has two distinct pathways, each of which is equally important: 1) acquiring the knowledge, and 2) cultivating the desire. We must know what it is we are seeking and then initiate the desire to find it. The phrase is admittedly easy to comprehend, but not so easy to execute.

The frustrating part for most people is that the desire for potential is built in—the motivation to develop is written into our DNA. We are all created for a purpose, so desire is part of our primal origins. The only curious difference is that some people actively pursue the ideal and some never seem to unearth it—for some, the desire remains dormant.

In the end, the active pursuit of the knowledge required to seek potential, and the unquenchable thirst of desire to accomplish their potential, is what distinguishes those who realize greatness from those who don't.

Wright

How do people start the journey of discovering their human potential? Give us a few ideas to get us moving in the right direction.

Gillum

The most difficult task that anyone undertakes in any project is the starting point. In writing, a blank page is the hardest obstacle to overcome, so writers developed a simple exercise called "stream-of-consciousness" writing that helps them get started. It makes no difference at all what they write about at first, just that they physically start moving the pen or tapping on the keyboard. Eventually, the action of movement overcomes the inertia of the blank page, and the brain-revving physical process engages the mental creative process, and meaningful writing emerges.

From a practical point of view, the journey of potential is largely an educational one. Just as humanists during the Renaissance looked back to antiquity for answers to their current problems, we can engage in the same process. We gain wisdom from the past if we let those lessons teach us. We can then use that information in the present to make better decisions, which consequently can lead us into a better future.

The humanists believed that their problems could be solved from a new educational system that stressed the similarities between Florence and ancient Rome. They called their educational system studia humanitatis, which means the "study of the humanities," or what it means to be human. They believed that for an individual to be successful, becoming citizens and participating in society was crucial. This participation was a direct result of their educational process that focused on the two primary sides of the human personality, one that focused on the intellect, or reasoning power, and the other focused on the will, or a person's desire. The intellect was educated by knowledge, or sapientia, while the will was formed through eloquentia, or the art of convincing through communication, a process they also referred to as rhetoric. In other words, success in society came from the knowledge of how to make good judgments and decisions about daily life, and the power and ability to then communicate and enact them effectively.

The same pattern still holds true today. Our success is dependent on our knowledge of a particular area of study and the ability to effectively communicate that knowledge to another person or into the world. The art of communicating ideas, whether oral, through the written word, or by some other vehicle has always, and will always be, a prerequisite of success in the world.

So if knowledge is where we begin, start reading. Although a relatively lost art today, reading is one of the most fundamental precursors to success. A recent research article in the Harvard Business Review reported that the number one trait that successful CEOs have in common is their focus on reading. And reading in many topical areas is better than just reading in one area of interest. The ability to take information from one field of study and apply that information in another field of study is one common avenue for innovation. This is a generalist philosophy, by in large, not a specialist mentality. But interestingly enough, over the last five or ten years, a trend in higher education is getting some attention. It is more difficult for students to get into MFA programs than MBA programs. Why? Companies are starting to realize that a broad, liberal arts education better serves the organization today in the information age. MBA programs build great business minds—but in this global society, a much broader education provides a better background. Therefore, we can learn much from studying other disciplines. In the end, reading builds competence, which then breeds confidence; and those inspired with confidence can be very successful in whatever they attempt. So goal number one is to start a reading program.

Secondly, once you begin to gain an appreciation for the scope of knowledge in your given subject area, begin the process of communicating that subject into the world. The process of expression or articulating a subject is, without question, the most important skill anyone can develop, especially leaders. You can know everything there is to know about the subject in question, but if you can't communicate the idea effectively to someone else, the power of the knowledge is lost. Through speaking, presenting, writing, blogging, acting, whatever the mode of transmission, getting a firm handle on how to communicate your ideas will effectively lead you to success in whatever area of life you want to develop. So goal number two is learning how to enhance your communication skills and how to articulate your ideas more effectively.

Wright

Human potential seems to be a big target to chase. How critical is it to study your own potential in a world that seems to be increasingly more fragmented and desensitized to individualism?

Gillum

Indeed, the focus of our world, especially in the corporate arena, seems to be on team dynamics. How do we as individuals contribute to the team? What are the dysfunctions of the team? How can managers sacrifice their own personal gain to allow their team to win? There is no "I" in team, right?

I think the idea that better fits the sign of the times is "unity through diversity." So how can we apply this concept to our quest for potential? As we are developing in each individual domain of life (e.g., physical, mental, social-emotional, or spiritual), a dynamic synthesis begins to occur when all four domains start "communicating," or acting in unity. That blending process is the fusion in humanfusion.

Let's look at an example. In the beginning stages, when someone starts organizing himself or herself (physical) and begins to focus (mental), achievement starts to occur. Additionally, when that same someone starts becoming aware of his or her strengths and challenges (social-emotional), and blends that with a sense of gratitude (spiritual); the person is now starting to gain a healthy perspective on what is possible for them. This person is now integrating all four domains simultaneously. When this happens, fusion occurs, and the blend we call autonomy. It's the first stage of fusion, and the first stage in exploring one's potential.

Fast-forwarding perhaps many years into the future, in the final development stages of each domain, four individual competencies blend together to form a synthesized impression of achievement we call renaissance. Managing energy (physical) is blended with genius (mental), and social intelligence (social-emotional) is merged with a sense of humility and joy (spiritual), and the archetypal Renaissance human is born. That's as close as we get to potential, and it's the greatest ride you can imagine.

Wright

The marketing tagline for the coaching division of humanfusion is "fusioncoaching—the renaissance of self." Your philosophy and worldview has been greatly influenced by the Italian Renaissance. What can be learned about our potential from studying this period of history?

Gillum

Renaissance Italy was the frontrunner of the "modern age," and a time when the rediscovery of the cultural heritage of ancient Greece and Rome led to an original way of looking at the world. They took lessons from the past and applied them to the problems of the present to enhance their future. This had not been done since antiquity. So what can we learn from this? By looking back with acuity, we can look forward with clarity. This is a very important concept for any student of personal development. By developing our skill of targeted reflection, we can better utilize our skill of visualizing our future, and thus our potential. This activity also has the collateral benefit of significantly increasing our outlook on optimism and personal happiness.

Let's look at how this works practically in more detail. Through my use of reflection over the last five years, I came to know that creativity was a very important value to me, and that one of the primary reasons I chose to leave the pharmaceutical industry was the increasing inability to be creative. So the underlying knowledge of how important creativity is to me can guide me to make better choices in the now, which will lead to more positive outcomes in my future. For example, if I know I have a certain amount of creative license in a project or new business venture, I will consider it, as long as it supports my mission and purpose. However, if I know from the beginning that creativity will be limited, then I can make a conscious choice not to get involved, since I know that only frustration will arise from suppressing my value around creativity. When I can make a decision that allows me to be creative, I thrive. I can work toward my potential and at the same time gain a greater sense of happiness and personal fulfillment.

The Italian Renaissance was an age of genius, a time when human beings reached new levels of self-expression. Not only did society undergo massive change, but the individual, for the first time in well over one thousand years, underwent a personal transformation—a personal renaissance—where the impetus to develop human potential was not only encouraged, it was in demand. This undeniable outpouring of individual creativity and the sheer magnitude of brilliance in Renaissance Italy makes it one of the great ages of human achievement. Similarly, we know that over the last seventy-five years there have been advances in science and technology that may allow the ages of information and industrialism to rival the achievements of the Renaissance. We will have to let future historians make that call.

Here's the interesting paradox: the Renaissance saw the emergence of the individual as seen rising through the fabric of society; the information age allows us to look at how society emerges as a reflection of individuals.

Wright

You left reasonably safe and secure jobs in academia and the pharmaceutical industry to pursue the entrepreneurial path, and specifically the path to become a business coach. What factors influenced your decision?

Gillum

Anytime you consider a life-altering choice of action, there seem to be a series of factors that converge in the juncture of decision-making that ultimately affect what you end up doing. Throughout the mid-nineties I was being heavily pursued by the pharmaceutical industry. Over the summer and fall of 1995 I had given a series of lectures for one company and really enjoyed working with their sales team. Their daily work habits operated on a very different energy level than I was used to, and it affected me in a way I had not expected. Not that my work habits were poor; they were simply different. I was very attracted to the thought of working in concert with very positive, high-performing, goal-oriented people every day—people who were really in pursuit of something. In literature, this would be called my foreshadowing—I was getting a different glimpse of the way other people managed energy, and that vision was a draft of the way I would come to manage my own.

Here is where the convergence of factors met—more like crashed—in the intersection of stimulus and response. Let me explain this a little more in detail. When Stephen Covey was conducting his research on The 7 Habits of Highly Effective People, he stumbled across a Hawaiian proverb that became important to the concept of Habit One concerning proactivity: Between stimulus and response there is a space. Within that space is our ability to choose our response. In that response is found our growth and our happiness. The profound implications of this concept are staggering. Whatever happens to us happens—our response to what happens to us is what makes all the difference. And the empowering principle that fuels our growth as humans is the inspiration that we can choose our response—no matter what happens to us. The secret lies in how we use the space—the space between what happens to us, or stimulus, and how we respond.

I was listening to the audiotape of the Seven Habits when this concept hit me like the lead pipe in the conservatory. It was that eight-hour drive in October 1995 between Virginia and Kentucky that really changed my life in a very dramatic way—a way that still has an incredible impact on me even today. I was teaching pharmacology at a very prestigious medical institution in Virginia, but I was unhappy. I found no fulfillment in what I was doing or trying to achieve. And to be fair, there was absolutely nothing wrong with the institution, but everything was wrong with me. I was simply trying to meet the expectations of my education, my mentor, my department, and my students. Unfortunately, what was totally missing from the equation was me and what I wanted to do with my life.

That's when the connection to proactivity hit me—the situation I was in was providing a stimulus that was leading me to complacency and mediocrity because I was not utilizing the space correctly. When I decided to use the space in a different way, one that honored me and what I wanted to achieve in life, determination and resolve around change surfaced in a new and powerful way. For the first time, I took complete control of my life, and it felt amazing. When I returned to Virginia I handed in my resignation and began my work with the pharmaceutical industry the very next month. It was that quick, and I was that sure. Once you have a very clear picture of what you need to do, you should waste no time doing it.

Consequently, the same sequence of stimulus-space-response led to my decision to leave the pharmaceutical industry and pursue my own vision. I now use the space for virtually every decision I make. If we maximize the use of the space between stimulus and response, we can take full advantage of our decisions to live on purpose and on mission, and live more fulfilling lives.

Wright

You also use metaphors to guide clients. Are there metaphors that complement and illuminate the idea of human potential?

Gillum

Mr. Shakespeare said that the entire world's a stage, and that men and women are merely players, having our entrances and exits. Shakespeare outlines human potential here in finite terms—we all get our cues, we strut about the stage for a period of time, and we finally make our exits; it's what we do with the time we have on stage that makes the difference. So the question becomes, as it relates to your own potential, what act is your play in? Do your scenes have an impact? Are you the author, or is someone else? What a brilliant use of metaphor to describe the human journey, which is why Shakespeare is considered pure genius. In this regard, literature and poetry become powerful vehicles for metaphors where, with a few words, emotions and associations from one context (human life) are connected with characteristics and entities of a different context (a stage).

In coaching, we use a variant called the therapeutic metaphor to help guide our clients through conceptual images of a situation that help them see their story paralleled in a different way—an insight that is hopefully more revealing to them. The purpose is to effectively highlight certain aspects or lessons of the current situation that otherwise might be lost or not as clearly perceived by the client or to illuminate entirely new perspectives on their situation.

In the poem The Journey by Mary Oliver, she describes the fateful decision of a person who has finally come to a realization that he or she must start taking control of his or her life. The poem parallels a dramatic life decision with that of a terrible storm. In many ways, the crisis in the situation, although we are unaware of what it is, becomes the beginning point in the search for potential. Once determination surfaces, look what happens—the voices start shouting, the house begins to tremble, the wind reaches out and pries with its stiff fingers, and the road is littered with branches and stones. You really get the picture. This decision of taking control of your life is not easy, and is inundated with many difficulties. But we know the storm will pass, the stars will eventually shine through the clouds; and our job is to firmly persevere, hold on to our resolve, and work to save the only life we can save—our own.

Metaphors give us vivid pictures. Metaphors throw brighter, more interesting light onto subjects we are struggling with. Metaphors give us rich images we can hold in our mind's eye long after the situation has aged, and in so doing, teach us long after the teacher has left the stage.

Wright

You utilize a number of mental models when you work with your clients. Why are they important?

Gillum

Most of us have a strong visual component to the way we learn and process information. I certainly do. So I use mental models perhaps because it is an extension of how I learn. One picture is worth how many words? Exactly—we can represent a complete philosophy by a single vision or picture. The basic tenets of Christianity reside on the death and resurrection of Christ, so the simple image of the cross can symbolically represent an entire doctrine vitally important to the Christian faith.

The circle is also a powerful model used in many disciplines. The circular logo of humanfusion mentioned before represents the process of continuous improvement, or kaizen. The metaphor of the circle reflects the idea that the process really has no clearly defined beginning or end—it's very difficult to know when we start the process, and when the process is over. Our system of growth and development includes elements that we revisit every day. That cycle allows us to refine and replace bad habits with better ones, and bad responses with better choices. The mental image of the circle can allow someone a powerful understanding of the journey of personal development.

The visual imagery of a river is another mental model that can represent the ebb and flow of human life. As humans, we are drawn to rivers—to moving water—perhaps because we are mostly composed of moving water, so perhaps there is a certain original connection we feel when we are around this elemental life source. The Greek philosopher, Heraclitus, said that we never step into the same river twice. The river is in constant motion, just like our physical bodies, so that once we step in, the very next second, both the river and our body have changed. This is a bit disconcerting sometimes—to understand that our body is constantly changing, and we are fundamentally different right now than when we started this interview.

So then, in what way is life like a river? Life is always moving forward; it has a beginning and an end; it starts small and gains the perspectives of width and depth as it progresses; life moves at varying speeds, flowing quickly at times, and stagnating at others; it floods and it trickles; it completely reacts to the forces around it. What a perfect metaphor the river provides for life. The key question is how do we handle the changes imposed on us by the river?

Wright

Are there role models of human potential—examples of people who have obtained the "holy grail" of potential?

Gillum

I think most people realize that it is rather naïve to think that any one human could achieve full potential. Brain researchers suggest that we are tapping into less than 10 percent of our total brain capacity. From the research on emotional intelligence (EQ) and leadership, the development of simply one-fourth of the EQ competencies that drive superior leadership performance will make you a superstar. No one would expect that a human could be so competent in all areas. So whether full potential is attainable or not should only be a question that amuses those of us who like to wax philosophical about life—it simply isn't an important goal to attain—it's good enough just to put up the target; the knowledge gained in the pursuit of potential is much more gratifying. And more importantly, everyone can get into the game of pursuit, and the subject matter is far from trivial.

Since the Italian Renaissance holds such fascination for me, let's consider just a few examples of people who contributed to this theory of why the Renaissance was considered one of the greatest creative periods in history. Francesco Petrarch, called the father of humanism, went against hundreds of years of conventional wisdom to inspire a new ideology that humans could take control of many aspects of their lives, and advocated a new education that would ultimately fuel the Renaissance. Giotto was the first to represent emotions in art, and show us our humanity through painting. Leonardo Da Vinci, Michelangelo, and Raphael produced arguably the greatest works of art in history. Lorenzo de' Medici developed a new level of sophistication in politics and practically invented the art of diplomacy. Machiavelli conceived political philosophy. Brunelleschi combined art and technology to create architectural structures we are still astonished by today.

And perhaps the greatest universal genius of the time was Leon Battista Alberti. When one thinks of the quintessential Renaissance man, Alberti is the first to come to mind. He was a painter, an architect, a scholar, and a theoretician of art. He wrote a Latin play in the Classical style before he was twenty. He was a brilliant organist, invented a machine that could raise sunken ships, and went to Rome to study architecture. He would later write a textbook on architecture modeled on Vitruvius. He wrote the first scientific treatise on painting, and wrote the first book ever published on home economics.

There are certainly many examples of people who have vigorously pursued the path of potential. However, the more interesting knowledge that develops when you look for role models is not the ultimate things they produced, but how they produced them. All of the people I have mentioned thus far had a major impact on the world, even though their collective "art" might have been in dissimilar subjects.

So what connects each of them? The one thing that is true of Renaissance men and women is an insatiable curiosity about life and everything in it. Think about someone who has changed the world in some way, and you will be thinking of someone who is or was always curious, testing boundaries, always shaking things up, and never satisfied with the status quo. A non-conforming attitude coupled with curiosity of how the world works is what fuels the creative engine that changes the world. The destination is gratifying, but the real value is in the messiness of the journey.

Wright

Sometimes I wonder if some people are born with a "renaissance" gene. Does one have to be born with certain superhuman powers or can potential be learned?

Gillum

Research from Dr. Martin Seligman's group from the University of Pennsylvania on what constitutes human happiness has some interesting data to look at in this regard. It turns out that about 50 percent of the factors that contribute to our "happiness" are completely out of our control. About half of your score on any happiness test is accounted for by what your biological parents would have scored had they taken the test. So there is a strong component of nature involved in our ability to lead happy lives.

The good news is that there is also another half to the story. Depending on our life experiences, we have an internal thermostat for happiness that has generated a baseline range of moods and emotions that make us feel more or less happy. Additionally, there are very specific variables that we have complete control over and if exercised, these can lead to statistically significant increases in happiness scores over time. The bottom line regarding happiness is this: we are governed by nature and by our parents, but equally true is our ability to control known factors that can make us intrinsically more happy and grateful over time.

The same is true for potential. There are certain characteristics and behavioral traits of humans that make them more susceptible to thrive on the road to success or wilt under its pressure. Most of these behaviors are imprinted in our younger days, and are relatively fixed by the time we graduate from college. So once you enter adulthood, your behavioral pattern is fairly consistent from that point on over time. The good news is, just like with happiness, there are certain variables that can set the stage for success or set the bar very high. Either way, behaviors that help drive higher levels of success in your life can be learned, and if implemented consistently over time, can result in sustained success.

Wright

You utilize questions in your coaching practice to guide your clients through transformational change. Can a simple question, or series of questions, be powerful tools for exploring potential?

Gillum

Absolutely, and of course the facetious response is "there's no question about it!" Questions are without a doubt the single most important tool that a coach utilizes in his or her practice of guiding clients through transformational change.

While in senior management with the pharmaceutical industry I was working with a coach to improve my management skills. One day I casually told him that I would love to do what he was doing every day—coach people to success. His response was "Why don't you?" It sounds trivial, but that changed everything—my thinking in that moment transformed from a thought process that had not considered the possibility of becoming a coach, to a thought process that allowed me to envision being a coach. In that moment all I could see was what was possible. And it was the clarity around the vision, and around the real possibilities of that vision, that fueled my desire to pursue my current path. And that would not have occurred to me in that moment without a simple, profoundly timed question.

As coaches, we need to understand the power and role that questions play. This power is the heart and soul of our practice, the fine-tuned art of asking the "ideal" question that allows people to see a future they had not imagined before. In the chaos of our everyday lives, thoughts and ideas compete with busyness, and it is the questions that demand our focus. Thoughtful questions allow us to dream and provide the fuel that can really energize a vision. Provocative questions break our current mental patterns, which allow us to innovate and create new associations that can lead to even greater invention. In the arena of knowledge work, questions occupy the space between "not knowing and our desire to know" where we are the most attentive, so that questions that are deeply compelling drive knowledge creation and expansion.

Therefore, real knowledge—real intellectual capital—emerges around the constructive use of questions. This fantastic place of discovery, going mentally at first, then physically, where you have never gone before, is the result of being open to the powerful process of questioning. In a world where understanding the paradox of unity and diversity is as important as ever, questions allow people to participate in the debate. Questions are vital; they keep us moving forward.

Wright

When does the journey of human potential begin? What happens along the way, and when does the journey conclude? Will we be rewarded for our efforts?

Gillum

The journey of potential can only begin when you are ready, when you truly accept the call to pursue your potential. All of us get the call to be a hero one day. It says, "Do something important. Do something significant with your life."

I teach my clients the story of the hero's journey by Joseph Campbell. It models the path we all must take to eventually see the world through a new lens—a lens you can only look through as a person who has been transformed by positive change. Campbell describes several stages the hero encounters along the way, organizing divisions into three sections: departure, initiation, and return. "Departure" deals with the hero beginning the journey, venturing forth on the quest. "Initiation" deals with the hero's encounters along the way. "Return" deals with the hero's return home with the accumulated knowledge and power acquired on the journey.

In the story, the hero starts in the ordinary world, and receives a call to begin the mythic voyage that must result in transformation or failure. If the hero accepts the call to enter the journey, he or she must face critical tasks and trials in the beginning, either alone or with assistance. As the journey reaches the point of greatest intensity, the hero must survive a severe challenge or the principle ordeal, often with help earned along the way. If the hero survives, the hero will achieve a great gift—the gift of transformation. Anyone who survives the principle ordeal cannot be the same person who entered it—he or she must be a new person, with new knowledge or insight not possessed before. The hero must then return to the ordinary world with this gift to educate others about the journey and in some way improve the world. Again, the privilege of leadership comes with the responsibility of education.

Wright

I assume we are going to bump into obstacles along this path. What happens if we turn back—if we neglect or ignore our potential?

Gillum

In the Hero's Journey, Joseph Campbell called this turning away the "refusal of the call." The universe is usually not kind to those who ignore their potential.

Since we all have a purpose—an intrinsic reason for being here—if we ignore our potential, then we are willingly evading our responsibility.

As humans, we have tremendous power. We have the ability to reason, to think creatively, to analyze information, and most importantly, to make choices. Think about it: we can choose to do anything we want to do; we simply need to focus our resolve on what we want and make it happen. How many stories do we hear about someone who has overcome immense odds to achieve something in his or her life? And how do stories like this happen? The person made a firm decision to change his or her circumstances, and nothing was going to get in the way.

This type of resolve reminds me of how Lady Macbeth encouraged her husband to "screw [your] courage to the sticking place, and we'll not fail." (Although, if you know the story, that task was for all of the wrong reasons.) Her words can still have an impact on our need to develop a strong sense of purpose and mission when we set out to accomplish anything important. Nothing gets in the way of determination once a decision is made to alter the status quo and seek a different path.

And as fairness would have it, we can just as easily choose to do nothing at all. Unfortunately, most of the time this is the choice that wins out; since it is the easier path to follow, it takes much less energy to go with the stream, to merge onto the road everyone else is taking. Humans follow energy. So we pick up on the momentum of that energy, even if the energy behind the motion is leading to complacency and mediocrity. Again, the road less traveled is aptly named for a very good reason—fewer take it because it requires more energy to travel on it.

Wright

Exploring your potential sounds like a ride worth taking. What rewards await those who are willing to accept the challenge?

Gillum

The reward process begins just by accepting the challenge—there is an uncanny knowing that forms in your mind and soul that anticipates your life is about to change. That knowledge is accompanied by a profound sense of well-being. The greatest reward on the road to potential is the intense sense of peace you experience when you know you are actively participating in something significant, something bigger than yourself. When you have given your personal mission and purpose statements time to form, time to incubate and refine over time, and when every action you take supports those targets, the universe has many advantages in store for you.

Often the most successful members of our society are on a path—a path that is leading them toward the pinnacle of development in four dimensions of being human: their mind, their body, their emotions, and their spirit. Their development is simultaneous, not one over the exclusion of the other. This human development is what fusion is all about, and is what lays the groundwork for human potential.

Searching for the holy grail of self-development will not yield a secret formula or ancient recipe; it will yield a process. There is no magic involved, only very hard work. There will be more invested than your time and resources; you will be investing in a foundation that will unlock your potential to be a human success story—a person who understands what human fusion can mean.

The unifying goal of Renaissance humans is to gain the elusive insight into what makes them most effective, what stirs their passion, and to discover where that source of energy resides that will fan the ember of potential that lies dormant within so many of us—the emergent insight that leads to personal renaissance—a reinvention of the soul that makes us uniquely human and uniquely capable of making a contribution.

The world holds your flame of potential. You have the match. All you must do is set yourself on fire.

About Dr. J. Gregory Gillum

Kentucky native Dr. J. Gregory Gillum, keynote speaker, author and acclaimed entrepreneur business coach, is the Chief Executive Officer of the humanfusion group of companies. As the lead executive coach and trainer, he specializes in leadership development applications, business performance coaching, emotional intelligence, and guiding transformational change in individuals and organizations. A frequent keynote speaker in the areas of human performance and potential, Dr. Gillum spent six years on the faculty of the Medical College of Virginia, and eight years in marketing and senior management with GlaxoSmithKline. He earned his doctorate from the University of Kentucky and his professional coaching credentials from the Coaches Training Institute in San Rafael, California. He lives with his wife and two children on a farm in the rolling hills of central Kentucky.

Dr. J. Gregory Gillum, CPCC, CRTA
Chief Executive Officer
humanfusion group of companies
669 Three Forks Road
Richmond, Kentucky 40475
859.625.0823
greg@humanfusion.com
www.humanfusion.com

Blueprint for Success

Chapter **Six**

An interview with...

Julie Maloney

David Wright (Wright)

Today we're talking with Julie Maloney. Julie is an executive coach with eighteen years of experience in leadership development and organizational change. She specializes in working with women leaders and leaders in transition, from "green" (high potentials) to "great" (high achievers). Her company, High Potential Executive Coaching, designs and delivers executive coaching and leadership training in Fortune 500 companies. Her past and present client list includes AT&T, The Coca-Cola Company, Merck & Company, Microsoft Corporation, Spectrum Health, and the University of Michigan. Julie is the co-author of a previous book on success, *Driven by Wellth: The 7 Essentials for Healthy, Sustainable Results in 21st Century Business and Leadership*.

Among Julie's unique talents clients cite: her strong business and organizational acumen; her solutions, which are perceptive, practical, and relevant; and her talent for facilitating client insights that lead to both immediate results and long-term positive change. She has a special gift for supporting and developing the whole person (professional and personal) in leaders navigating the turbulent whitewaters of life and work in corporations.

Julie, this is a topic that you are personally and professionally passionate about. You believe that work/life balance is the new "gold standard" of success. What do you mean by that?

Julie Maloney (Maloney)

We live in a world literally obsessed with external success—with always achieving and having more. So I don't think money and titles and power have completely disappeared as measures of winners and losers. But what I have noticed is that work/life balance (WLB) has become the new gold standard—the new gold medal—in the survival Olympics of modern society.

WLB is the ultimate status marker of having "made it" and of "having it all." WLB is personified by the young professional who seamlessly blends his job in technology with his passion for competitive cycling, the executive dad leaving a meeting early, proudly stating that he's off to coach his teenage daughter's soccer team, or the accounting firm partner/mother of three who negotiates an 80 percent work schedule. She has made partner and made being a mom work for her. She's there for her clients and there to pick up her kids at school at the end of each day. So WLB is literally success on your own terms—a conscious choice to chart your own course and set your own standards.

In that sense, I think WLB is an incredibly sane and healthy evolution in our understanding of what constitutes a successful life. However, WLB as a measure of success also brings a unique challenge. By nature, WLB is transitory. You can't save it for a rainy day or put it in the bank. Just as soon as you think you have it, it begins to shift and slip away again. Like competing for an Olympic medal, there are times when you end up on the winner's stand with a bronze, silver, or gold medal. But you can't stay on that stand forever—eventually you have to get back into the race. And even medal winners must return to the starting line with everyone else.

Wright

So what are the implications of that highly individualized and transitory nature of work/life balance?

Maloney

When money is the measure, success is pretty clear (you either are a millionaire or you're not). But WLB is an extremely elusive thing to quantify because it is not a thing. WLB is a very personal experience of your own life and career. And no one can define the ideal experience for you, but you.

Yet, read most of the self-improvement and career/business success books that regularly populate the best-seller lists and you'll find strikingly similar formulas and advice. We've got a one-size-fits-all kind of approach to what has become a highly customized journey. The analogy here is that in the era of iPods it is as though we're all still listening to broadcast radio. So at best, we're defaulting to methods to find happiness and success that may or may not really fit our particular needs and dreams. At worst, this expert advice may actually be taking us—you or me, personally—in the wrong direction.

Wright

You talk about work/life balance being the right territory, but we're using the wrong maps. Would you tell our readers more about that?

Maloney

When it comes to success, WLB is absolutely the right territory for our modern era. Nothing else offers a more sustainable source for finding well-being, accomplishment, riches, joy, meaning, and fulfillment in our crazy-busy, 24/7 world. But we're using old maps to chart our path across constantly shifting territory. Take that a step further even—the very means and ways we are going after WLB are actually sabotaging the end results we hope to achieve.

Let me explain this another way. I was born and raised in the South, and my family roots are here in the farmland of the Midwest. Somewhere in that rural and often colorful history is an old joke that rings true to this point. A city slicker in a sports car speeds into a gas station in the middle of nowhere, totally lost. Late for his meeting and with barely a "hello" out of his mouth, he asks the station attendant for directions. The station attendant, leaning back in his chair, listens to the city slicker's harried request. After a few moments of silent consideration, the attendant firmly replies, "Sorry fella—you can't get there from here."

We live in a world where we are constantly wired by technology, caffeine, stress, and adrenaline. We tell ourselves all this facilitates our moving faster, smarter, and more efficiently because, as our logic goes, speed and efficiency are what maximize our work time so that we can get home to the rest of our lives. Yet for all of our productivity, we're still logging on all hours of the day and night and packing our laptops along with our suitcases for that brief, once-a-year vacation.

So we're actually not getting there from here—though we think we are. We're not being recharged and not finding peace and relaxation despite all our well-intentioned juggling. Leaning down from the lawn mower to sniff a rose in passing is not the same as stopping to smell the flowers.

The benefits that WLB brings can only be realized in the actual enjoyment of it—in the actual experience of it. This requires that we periodically step away from the frenetic rat race and cultivate a rhythm all our own. That means balancing our constant movement and drive forward with regular moments of simply being where we are.

Put another way, we actually have to be here to get there.

Wright

Be here to get there. That's a catchy phrase and certainly rings true on an intuitive level. Is that another way of talking about what you call the "yin and yang" of success?

Maloney

Yes, absolutely. In a world where the cycle of wanting and working never ends, we have to create our own stopping points. Otherwise, the wheel will keep on turning and eventually mow us down. The easiest way to success is to periodically stop and deeply experience the fruits of what we have already accomplished. This resting and recharging in what we have done then becomes the catalyst, the focus, the energy, and the enthusiasm required to jump back in the game.

From this perspective, true success is an inner experience of ease and fulfillment around one's external accomplishments. This is the yin/yang of success—the being and the doing. It is the dynamic interplay of energies that science and spiritual traditions alike tell us is the creative nature of all living things.

I am a practitioner of Zen Buddhism. In Buddhism, there are figures very similar to Catholic saints (the religion I was raised in). Kwan Yin is one of the most beloved of these Buddhist figures and she is revered worldwide as the embodiment of the female/yin energy. She is most famously depicted in a pose whose name I just adore, called "Royal Ease." Royal Ease is the image of a lovely woman, sitting in a relaxed and open way, yet supremely confident and filled with energy. This pose conveys tremendous power, even though she is just sitting. By pausing to not be in action, she is rested, alert, and ready for action when the right time comes.

This is so simple but so very important to understand. Inaction and action, being and doing all work together, feed each other, keep the ball rolling, and the momentum going. How does this happen? Think about a woman pregnant with a child. The process of bringing a new life into the world begins and ends with taking action—one pleasurable and the other often painful. But in between the actions is a relatively long period of inaction that is absolutely vital to the successful birth of a child. This is a time when the woman cannot "do" anything to make the baby arrive faster than the nine months required. Her best bet (in terms of the baby) is to just be with the process and try to rest in preparation for the birth. Our society is driven by a pervasive and hidden myth that doing alone produces results in this world, but success requires resting and doing—both.

Wright

You say that our global obsession with success is actually hiding a crisis of motivation. But I don't know anyone who isn't motivated to succeed in one-way or another. How does motivation play into this?

Maloney

Our global drive for success has led to an explosion of self-improvement, career, and money-focused books on creating the perfect life. If you spend time with this body of writing, you begin to see that the primary focus is on what to do and how to think (which is just another form of action). And most of these recommendations are not new, but have been around in some form or another for a really long time. Why then are so many of us still struggling with and/or searching for success?

I don't believe it is because we don't know what to do. In fact, most of us are wildly creative and exceptionally talented when it comes to taking action. What really gets in our way is a crisis of motivation.

I know it sounds weird. Who isn't motivated to succeed?

When it comes to success, the motivation part is always assumed. We all want wealth, fame, joy, love, accomplishments, and the good life—right? What is there to question in that? As a coach, I believe there is a fundamental question that is easily missed. That question is, are you chasing success or is failure chasing you?

Most of what drives people to succeed is actually not a desire for success itself as much as an attempt to avoid pain and suffering and failure. Yet pain, suffering, and failure are intrinsic to the human condition. So here's what most success books don't say: no matter how good you get at affirmations, positive thinking, doing all the right things in your career and your relationships, you're not going to avoid what's difficult in life. It's the two-sided coin you pay for the privilege of living; you don't get happiness without sadness, light without dark, winning without losing—at least some of the time.

As a result, we're all running around trying to avoid suffering versus actually experiencing success. "Avoiding suffering" and "being successful" are not the same, though we often forget and treat them as though they are. I've found that we have tremendous power to create WLB (or any other form of success we want) if we will make a simple but courageous choice. The choice is to practice living in the positive energy that comes from creating and enjoying and learning from our success. The alternative is to live literally driven by your fears instead of your dreams. Ultimately, fear results in limited choices and ineffective actions, as we try to avoid what might hurt or go wrong or, God forbid, fail. So this choice is no small thing to make and it can only be made in the one moment in time that is under your control—the present moment.

Wright

Speaking to the role of the present moment, many people who are looking for success are focused on what's next, where they want to be, or what they want to have in the future. What does success have to do with the now?

Maloney

I believe that we have access to a form of salvation here on earth. We can be reborn into the sweetness of our lives through our awareness of any given moment. Most of humanity is missing out on the most simple and essential ingredient for success that is right under our noses—the personal, self-created internal experience of joy, well-being, and accomplishment—achieved by simply by pausing long enough to notice what's going right and experiencing a taste of our success, in the moment. It is important to do this because something is always going right. I want to say that again—in any given moment, something is always going right. When you're obsessed with perceived failures in the past or with what you want to do or be better in the future, you totally miss where you are. Where you are may in fact be closer than you think to your dream or goal.

For a simple example, maybe you have a goal to be actively involved in your kids' lives. And for the last few weeks, you haven't made one of your son's soccer games. But in this moment he's in the kitchen with you, helping you get dinner on the table, and talking about his day with you. What experience are you having now? What is going right, right now?

Our thoughts literally form connections in our brains, like the roots and branches of trees. Focusing on what is going right is like shining the sun on the positive trees that grow in our brains (and keeping the light away from the negative ones). Either way, you're going to have a forest, but you have incredible choice around what kind of forest thrives there. Internally noticing and cultivating our positive experiences (however small) is much more than just celebrating the fruits of our labors or even being grateful for our blessings. (I don't mean to diminish gratitude. Gratitude is like fertilizer—it accelerates whatever it touches.) I'm talking about taking the first step of planting the seed itself—the acorn of your actual experience. That acorn will become a mighty oak if you make a little time to find it and tap it down into the soil. Remember the power of combining action and inaction? Your job is to start the process and periodically water and fertilize, but then all that is required is for you to step back and let the seed take on a life of its own.

Wright

So bring this back to work/life balance. It seems there is an element of self-empowerment in what you're talking about here, in noticing the success of any given moment.

Maloney

Very much so. When you take time to experience your success in any given moment, you are creating the conditions for even more success in the future. And it can happen in two different ways: First, you get to experience now the very reasons why you're bothering to work so hard in the first place. You get to have a taste (or more) of that balance and success today, not twenty years from now. While the formula of WLB for each person differs, this is the soil from which any form of WLB springs, because when you notice some of the payoff, you get recharged. You experience the enjoyment, energy, and motivation that brings personal fulfillment to your life now and the fuel for the fire to move on to what's next.

Second, when you pause to reflect on what's going right, you also have the opportunity to notice what got you here. To listen to and reflect on the great feedback you received from your customer last week or what that Little League trophy means to the team you just coached to a winning season. You get to take a moment to discover what you're really, really good at and how you made a difference in your company or for your family. By becoming more aware of the gifts that got you here, you can use them to create even more success. You get the confidence in your unique talents and passions to apply them somewhere new or somewhere you never thought of before.

Pausing to notice what success is already present in your life and experiencing it deeply doesn't have to take a lot of time. But practiced regularly, it can take us directly to the heart of work/life balance and to every other version of success we could dream up for ourselves. After all, isn't this inner experience the very reason why we're chasing all the other stuff (the title, the salary, the nice car, the big house, the vacation home, the relationship, etc.) to begin with? Those external things are supposed to deliver the inner experience. But, in and of themselves, they cannot. We have to take time to activate the joys they bring. To find work/life balance, we have to stop fast forwarding past our lives.

Wright

Why do you say women especially are challenged by this tendency to fast forward past their lives?

Maloney

It is not that men don't fast forward. Being a woman and having two daughters myself and working a great deal with women leaders, I'm just tuned into this particular expression of an equal opportunity struggle. We're so busy and so demanding on ourselves that we barely even look up at the home runs we keep delivering, time and time again. Life is throwing curve balls at a blinding speed and we're knocking them out of the park at the same time that we're chairing a business meeting, putting together our daughter's Girl Scout outing and planning what's for dinner.

While it's far from a perfect world out there, women are succeeding as never before. As the COO of the home and the CEO at work, we're doing more than ever before. It is stating the obvious to say that we're trying to be it all, do it all, and do it really well. So we're not taking the time to celebrate and enjoy what we've accomplished. Why is that? No, really—why? I know all the usual reasons. I've said them myself and lived them myself, the biggest one being that there's just no time. But I'm not buying that one any more.

If you look deeper, there is a more subtle, more insidious barrier to women recharging our own resources and rediscovering our own fulfillment, vitality, and joy. We have a habit of collapsing together two interpretations of any situation where something went wrong; we equate "life got hard" with "I failed." When, despite our best efforts, a ball gets dropped or we make a mistake (big or small), we are hard as the devil on ourselves.

As a result, we can live in a never-ending state of internal failure—a state of not experiencing in our hearts and souls the amazing results our minds and bodies created. In fact, I am convinced that no one is harder on a woman than she is on herself. Ask a woman what she is doing really well in a particular moment and nine times out of ten she'll reply with a list of things she's not doing well or should be doing better. The reason for this is that as a gender we have bought into the myth that true success means that we are smart enough or talented enough to bypass any struggles that might come our way. We forget that life is meant to be hard, as well as wonderful; maybe because it is in the toughest times that we tend to learn the most. There will be events in the course of our lives and careers that we simply cannot control and times when we will be unable to achieve what we want. And no amount of "being perfect" on our part is going to change the score.

That may sound on the surface like fatalism or giving up, but it is actually a very powerful shift in perspective. Giving ourselves a break gives us some breathing room—a degree of freedom to let go of judgment of a particular situation, of other people, and especially of ourselves. Only then can we give ourselves the emotional and psychological space required to remember that the goal is not to be perfect but rather to leverage what you have already got going for you. This is like climbing to the top of a fire tower—only when you get yourself up above the smoke can you see a broader vista and strategize from a place of strength how to fight any fire that comes your way.

Wright

How did you come to this understanding of work/life balance and success?

Maloney

I've worked in the field of leadership development for eighteen years and I've coached executives for over a decade. My beliefs around the power of finding your own rhythm come from both a wealth of professional experience and my own personal struggles and learning. About five years ago, everything in my life seemed to be falling apart at once at home and in my business. There was so much I had on my plate to deal with that I could barely stay on top of it. I felt like a total failure. I knew I was suffering for lack of time to step away from the craziness, but felt I couldn't afford to take the time for me. As a result, I found myself becoming physically, emotionally, and spiritually sick with stress.

So I started small, making dates with myself for just a half hour, once a week—time where I could just be, or think, or get my arms around a bigger picture of my life and work. I'd meditate, walk, read, journal, or go to a coffee shop, whatever I felt like doing. While it doesn't sound like much, I began to notice a difference in me. I was less stressed, more calm in dealing with challenges, able to focus better, and even finding my sense of humor again. I naturally found myself wanting more of that time and began to make it a priority to increase the down time (being time) in my life. Like the acorn I talked about earlier, that being time has grown into a very large oak tree of regularly scheduled time just for me, with amazing results in my life and my business. And I'm not done growing it yet!

Wright

So bottom-line this for us. What does the rhythm of success really mean?

Maloney

The secret to work/life balance and to success of any kind is to create your own rhythm of being and doing. It starts with taking moments to connect with the success you already have (taking time to notice and be with what's going right) so that you return to action motivated, rested and focused on your strengths. Even with the most tightly scheduled calendar, it doesn't have to take a lot of time to pause and find your own acorns—you can do it in a five-minute reflection at the start or end of every day. The most important thing is to start and practice it regularly for a time and notice what happens.

Wright

You have a self-coaching exercise you recommend to your clients to help them get started. Would you share that with us?

Maloney

Gladly! I ask women to take themselves on a micro-retreat for thirty to sixty minutes of uninterrupted quiet time alone. Even the busiest of my clients have never turned down that homework assignment; they can't wait to start and they find the time with surprising speed. You can use the self-coaching questions I'll give you in a moment to guide you. In fact, this particular exercise was designed for and is dedicated to my personal heroines—the women professionals, executives, and entrepreneurs who have also chosen to be spouses and mothers. You have literally taken on the whole world. I hope this gives you something back.

Try this exercise once a week for one month and see what happens. Then send me an e-mail (julie@greentogreat.com). I'd love to know what you found out.

Self-Coaching Exercise

You will need a computer or journal where you can write down your answers. For thirty to sixty minutes of uninterrupted quiet time alone (ideally in a place that is inspiring, beautiful, or peaceful to you) reflect on the five questions below. Write down your answers.

In answering the first question, focus on the qualities or values that define the deepest meaning of success for you (e.g., being an inspiration to my team or teaching my kids to be strong and independent) versus a specific objective (e.g., I am promoted to vice president by next year or I will make it to every soccer game my son has this season). If you can only come up with specific objectives to start, take a few extra minutes to ask yourself on each objective: "why do I want that?" until you get to an underlying value or inner experience that objective represents to you.

Reflection Questions
1. How do I define success?
2. What, in that definition of success, is here for me right now?
3. How am I enjoying/celebrating/experiencing my success? (If I'm not, how will I within the next forty-eight hours?)
4. What is it within me that made these particular successes a reality (my acorns)?
5. Resting here in my past success, what do I want now (my next goal)?
6. Identify three specific actions you will take this week toward your goal.

Just notice, over a few weeks or one month, how you feel and what happens in your life and work. Keep a written record of your answers and what you notice changing in your life or at your job. You may find yourself scheduling even bigger chunks of down time with yourself or new ways to celebrate the successes in your life. Or you may start to see certain strengths and skills that have served you in one area of your life or work are incredible assets in helping you achieve a goal another area.

If you find yourself getting stuck or having trouble with any part of this exercise, find a good coach to work with you. Sometimes all it takes is a few good questions from someone else to crack open the seed of change.

About Julie Maloney...

JULIE MALONEY is an executive coach with eighteen years of corporate experience in leadership development and organizational change. She specializes in working with women leaders and leaders in transition, from "green" (high potentials) to "great" (high achievers). Her company, High Potential Executive Coaching, designs and delivers executive coaching and leadership training in Fortune 500 companies.

Julie holds an MA in Sociology from Brown University and a BA in Sociology from Loyola University of New Orleans. She received her coach training from the Coaches Training Institute (CTI) and is a certified coach and member of the International Coach Federation (ICF). Julie's leadership background includes management and executive positions in The Coca-Cola Company, Ernst & Young, and entrepreneurial start-ups. Julie is the co-author of a previous book on success, *Driven by Wellth: The 7 Essentials for Healthy, Sustainable Results in 21st Century Business and Leadership.*

A native of Atlanta, Georgia, Julie resides in Ann Arbor, Michigan, with her husband and two daughters. A recovering over-achiever, Julie finds her rhythm for success through loving her work and stopping regularly to enjoy old passions: family, friendship, home, nature travel, hiking and snowshoeing, and new ones: photography and writing.

Julie Maloney
High Potential Executive Coaching
A division of Julie Maloney, Inc.
734.998.1110
julie@greentogreat.com
www.greentogreat.com

Chapter Seven

An interview with...

Dr. Kenneth Blanchard

David E. Wright (Wright)

Few people have created a positive impact on the day-to-day management of people and companies more than Dr. Kenneth Blanchard. He is known around the world simply as Ken, a prominent, gregarious, sought-after author, speaker, and business consultant. Ken is universally characterized by friends, colleagues, and clients as one of the most insightful, powerful, and compassionate men in business today. Ken's impact as a writer is far-reaching. His phenomenal best-selling book, *The One Minute Manager*, co-authored with Spencer Johnson, has sold more than thirteen million copies worldwide and has been translated into more than twenty-five languages. Ken is Chairman and "Chief Spiritual Officer" of the Ken Blanchard Companies. The organization's focus is to energize organizations around the world with customized training in bottom-line business strategies based on the simple, yet powerful principles inspired by Ken's best-selling books.

Dr. Blanchard, welcome to *Blueprint for Success*.

Dr. Ken Blanchard (Blanchard)

Well, it's nice to talk with you, David. It's good to be here.

Wright

I must tell you that preparing for your interview took quite a bit more time than usual. The scope of your life's work and your business, the Ken Blanchard Companies, would make for a dozen fascinating interviews.

Before we dive into the specifics of some of your projects and strategies, will you give our readers a brief synopsis of your life—how you came to be the Ken Blanchard we all know and respect?

Blanchard

Well, I'll tell you, David, I think life is what you do when you are planning on doing something else. I think that was John Lennon's line. I never intended to do what I have been doing. In fact, all my professors in college told me that I couldn't write. I wanted to do college work, which I did, and they said, "You had better be an administrator." So I decided I was going to be a Dean of Students. I got provisionally accepted into my master's degree program and then provisionally accepted at Cornell because I never could take any of those standardized tests.

I took the college boards four times and finally got 502 in English. I don't have a test-taking mind. I ended up in a university in Athens, Ohio, in 1966 as an Administrative Assistant to the Dean of the Business School. When I got there he said, "Ken, I want you to teach a course. I want all my deans to teach." I had never thought about teaching because they said I couldn't write, and teachers had to publish. He put me in the manager's department.

I've taken enough bad courses in my day and I wasn't going to teach one. I really prepared and had a wonderful time with the students. I was chosen as one of the top ten teachers on the campus coming out of the chute!

I just had a marvelous time. A colleague by the name of Paul Hersey was chairman of the Management Department. He wasn't very friendly to me initially because the Dean had led me to his department, but I heard he was a great teacher. He taught Organizational Behavior and Leadership. So I said, "Can I sit in on your course next semester?"

"Nobody audits my courses," he said. "If you want to take it for credit, you're welcome."

I couldn't believe it. I had a doctoral degree and he wanted me to take his course for credit—so I signed up.

The registrar didn't know what to do with me because I already had a doctorate, but I wrote the papers and took the course, and it was great.

In June 1967, Hersey came into my office and said, "Ken, I've been teaching in this field for ten years. I think I'm better than anybody, but I can't write. I'm a nervous wreck, and I'd love to write a textbook with somebody. Would you write one with me?"

I said, "We ought to be a great team. You can't write and I'm not supposed to be able to, so let's do it!"

Thus began this great career of writing and teaching. We wrote a textbook called *Management of Organizational Behavior: Utilizing Human Resources*. It came out in its eighth edition October 3, 2000 and the ninth edition was published September 3, 2007. It has sold more than any other textbook in that area over the years. It's been over forty years since that book first came out.

I quit my administrative job, became a professor, and ended up working my way up the ranks. I got a sabbatical leave and went to California for one year twenty-five years ago. I ended up meeting Spencer Johnson at a cocktail party. He wrote children's books— wonderful series called *Value Tales for Kids.* He also wrote *The Value of Courage: The Story of Jackie Robinson* and *The Value of Believing In Yourself: The Story Louis Pasteur.*

My wife, Margie, met him first and said, "You guys ought to write a children's book for managers because they won't read anything else." That was my introduction to Spencer. So, *The One Minute Manager* was really a kid's book for big people. That is a long way from saying that my career was well planned.

Wright

Ken, what and/or who were your early influences in the areas of business, leadership, and success? In other words, who shaped you in your early years?

Blanchard

My father had a great impact on me. He was retired as an admiral in the Navy and had a wonderful philosophy. I remember when I was elected as president of the seventh grade, and I came home all pumped up. My father said, "Son, it's great that you're the president of the seventh grade, but now that you have that leadership position, don't ever use it." He said, "Great leaders are followed because people respect them and like them, not because they have power." That was a wonderful lesson for me early on. He was just a great model for me. I got a lot from him.

Then I had this wonderful opportunity in the mid 1980s to write a book with Norman Vincent Peale. He wrote *The Power of Positive Thinking*. I met him when he was eighty-six years old; we were asked to write a book on ethics together, *The Power of Ethical Management: Integrity Pays, You Don't Have to Cheat to Win*. It didn't matter what we were writing together, I learned so much from him. He just built from the positive things I learned from my mother.

My mother said that when I was born I laughed before I cried, I danced before I walked, and I smiled before I frowned. So that, as well as Norman Vincent Peale, really impacted me as I focused on what I could do to train leaders. How do you make them positive? How do you make them realize that it's not about them, it's about who they are serving? It's not about their position—it's about what they can do to help other people win.

So, I'd say my mother and father, then Norman Vincent Peale. All had a tremendous impact on me.

Wright

I can imagine. I read a summary of your undergraduate and graduate degrees. I assumed you studied Business Administration, marketing management, and related courses. Instead, at Cornell you studied Government and Philosophy. You received your master's from Colgate in Sociology and Counseling and your PhD from Cornell in Educational Administration and Leadership. Why did you choose this course of study? How has it affected your writing and consulting?

Blanchard

Well, again, it wasn't really well planned out. I originally went to Colgate to get a master's degree in Education because I was going to be a Dean of Students over men. I had been a Government major, and I was a Government major because it was the best department at Cornell in the Liberal Arts School. It was exciting. We would study what the people were doing at the league of governments. And then, the Philosophy Department was great. I just loved the philosophical arguments. I wasn't a great student in terms of getting grades, but I'm a total learner. I would sit there and listen, and I would really soak it in.

When I went over to Colgate and got into the education courses, they were awful. They were boring. The second week, I was sitting at the bar at the Colgate Inn saying, "I can't believe I've been here two years for this." This is just the way the Lord works: Sitting next to me in the bar was a young sociology professor who had just gotten his PhD at Illinois. He was staying at the Inn. I was moaning and groaning about what I was doing, and he said, "Why don't you come and major with me in sociology? It's really exciting."

"I can do that?" I asked.

He said, "Yes."

I knew they would probably let me do whatever I wanted the first week. Suddenly, I switched out of Education and went with Warren Ramshaw. He had a tremendous impact on me. He retired some years ago as the leading professor at Colgate in the Arts and Sciences, and got me interested in leadership and organizations. That's why I got a master's in Sociology.

The reason I went into educational administration and leadership? It was a doctoral program I could get into because I knew the guy heading up the program. He said, "The greatest thing about Cornell is that you will be in the School of Education. It's not very big, so you don't have to take many education courses, and you can take stuff all over the place."

There was a marvelous man by the name of Don McCarty who eventually became the Dean of the School of Education, Wisconsin. He had an impact on my life; but I was always just searching around.

My mission statement is: to be a loving teacher and example of simple truths that help myself and others to awaken the presence of God in our lives. The reason I mention "God" is that I believe the biggest addiction in the world is the human ego; but I'm really into simple truth. I used to tell people I was trying to get the B.S. out of the behavioral sciences.

Wright

I can't help but think, when you mentioned your father, that he just bottom-lined it for you about leadership.

Blanchard

Yes.

Wright

A man named Paul Myers, in Texas, years and years ago when I went to a conference down there, said, "David, if you think you're a leader and you look around, and no one is following you, you're just out for a walk."

Blanchard

Well, you'd get a kick out of this—I'm just reaching over to pick up a picture of Paul Myers on my desk. He's a good friend, and he's a part of our Center for FaithWalk Leadership where we're trying to challenge and equip people to lead like Jesus. It's non-profit. I tell people I'm not an evangelist because we've got enough trouble with the Christians we have. We don't need any more new ones. But, this is a picture of Paul on top of a mountain. Then there's another picture below that of him under the sea with stingrays. It says, "Attitude is everything. Whether you're on the top of the mountain or the bottom of the sea, true happiness is achieved by accepting God's promises, and by having a biblically positive frame of mind. Your attitude is everything." Isn't that something?

Wright

He's a fine, fine man. He helped me tremendously. In keeping with the theme of our book, *Blueprint for Success,* I wanted to get a sense from you about your own success journey. Many people know you best from *The One Minute Manager* books you coauthored with Spencer Johnson. Would you consider these books as a high water mark for you or have you defined success for yourself in different terms?

Blanchard

Well, you know, *The One Minute Manager* was an absurdly successful book so quickly that I found I couldn't take credit for it. That was when I really got on

102

my own spiritual journey and started to try to find out what the real meaning of life and success was.

That's been a wonderful journey for me because I think, David, the problem with most people is they think their self-worth is a function of their performance plus the opinion of others. The minute you think that is what your self-worth is, every day your self-worth is up for grabs because your performance is going to fluctuate on a day-to-day basis. People are fickle. Their opinions are going to go up and down. You need to ground your self-worth in the unconditional love that God has ready for us, and that really grew out of the unbelievable success of *The One Minute Manager*.

When I started to realize where all that came from, that's how I got involved in this ministry that I mentioned. Paul Myers is a part of it. As I started to read the Bible, I realized that everything I've ever written about, or taught, Jesus did. You know, He did it with the twelve incompetent guys He "hired." The only guy with much education was Judas, and he was His only turnover problem.

Wright

Right.

Blanchard

This is a really interesting thing. What I see in people is not only do they think their self-worth is a function of their performance plus the opinion of others, but they measure their success on the amount of accumulation of wealth, on recognition, power, and status. I think those are nice success items. There's nothing wrong with those, as long as you don't define your life by that.

What I think you need to focus on rather than success is what Bob Buford, in his book *Halftime,* calls "significance"—moving from success to significance. I think the opposite of accumulation of wealth is generosity.

I wrote a book called *The Generosity Factor* with Truett Cathy who is the founder of Chick-fil-A. He is one of the most generous men I've ever met in my life. I thought we needed to have a model of generosity. It's not only your *treasure,* but it's your *time* and *talent*. Truett and I added *touch* as a fourth one.

The opposite of recognition is service. I think you become an adult when you realize you're here to serve rather than to be served.

Finally, the opposite of power and status is loving relationships. Take Mother Teresa as an example—she couldn't have cared less about recognition, power, and status because she was focused on generosity, service, and loving relationships; but she got all of that earthly stuff. If you focus on the earthly, such as money, recognition, and power, you're never going to get to significance. But if you focus on significance, you'll be amazed at how much success can come your way.

Wright

I spoke with Truett Cathy recently and was impressed by what a down-to-earth, good man he seems to be. When you start talking about him closing his restaurants on Sunday, all of my friends—when they found out I had talked to him—said, "Boy, he must be a great Christian man, but he's rich." I told them, "Well, to put his faith into perspective, by closing on Sunday it costs him $500 million a year."

He lives his faith, doesn't he?

Blanchard

Absolutely, but he still outsells everybody else.

Wright

That's right.

Blanchard

According to their January 25, 2007, press release, Chick-fil-A was the nation's second-largest quick-service chicken restaurant chain in sales at that time. Its business performance marks the thirty-ninth consecutive year the chain has enjoyed a system-wide sales gain—a streak the company has sustained since opening its first chain restaurant in 1967.

Wright

The simplest market scheme, I told him, tripped me up. I walked by his first Chick-fil-A I had ever seen, and some girl came out with chicken stuck on toothpicks and handed me one; I just grabbed it and ate it, it's history from there on.

Blanchard

Yes, I think so. It's really special. It is so important that people understand generosity, service, and loving relationships because too many people are running around like a bunch of peacocks. You even see pastors who measure their success by how many in are in their congregation; authors by how many books they have sold; businesspeople by what their profit margin is—how good sales are. The reality is that's all well and good, but I think what you need to focus on is the other. I think if business did that more and we got Wall Street off our backs with all the short-term evaluation, we'd be a lot better off.

Wright

Absolutely. There seems to be a clear theme that winds through many of your books that have to do with success in business and organizations—how people are treated by management and how they feel about their value to a company. Is this an accurate observation? If so, can you elaborate on it?

Blanchard

Yes, it's a very accurate observation. See, I think the profit is the applause you get for taking care of your customers and creating a motivating environment for your people. Very often people think that business is only about the bottom line. But no, that happens to be the result of creating raving fan customers, which I've described with Sheldon Bowles in our book, *Raving Fans*. Customers want to brag about you, if you create an environment where people can be gung-ho and committed. You've got to take care of your customers and your people, and then your cash register is going to go ka-ching, and you can make some big bucks.

Wright

I noticed that your professional title with the Ken Blanchard Companies is somewhat unique—"Chairman and Chief Spiritual Officer." What does your title mean to you personally and to your company? How does it affect the books you choose to write?

Blanchard

I remember having lunch with Max DuPree one time. The legendary Chairman of Herman Miller, Max wrote a wonderful book called *Leadership Is an Art.*

"What's your job?" I asked him.

He said, "I basically work in the vision area."

"Well, what do you do?" I asked.

"I'm like a third grade teacher," he replied. "I say our vision and values over, and over, and over again until people get it right, right, right."

I decided from that, I was going to become the Chief Spiritual Officer, which means I would be working in the vision, values, and energy part of our business. I ended up leaving a morning message every day for everybody in our company. We have twenty-eight international offices around the world.

I leave a voice mail every morning, and I do three things on that as Chief Spiritual Officer: One, people tell me who we need to pray for. Two, people tell me who we need to praise—our unsung heroes and people like that. And then three, I leave an inspirational morning message. I really am the cheerleader—the Energizer Bunny—in our company. I'm the reminder of why we're here and what we're trying to do.

We think that our business in the Ken Blanchard Companies is to help people lead at a higher level, and to help individuals and organizations. Our mission statement is to unleash the power and potential of people and organizations for the common good. So if we are going to do that, we've really got to believe in that.

I'm working on getting more Chief Spiritual Officers around the country. I think it's a great title and we should get more of them.

Wright

So those people for whom you pray, where do you get the names?

Blanchard

The people in the company tell me who needs help, whether it's a spouse who is sick or kids who are sick or if they are worried about something. We've got over five years of data about the power of prayer, which is pretty important.

One morning, my inspirational message was about my wife and five members of our company who walked sixty miles one weekend—twenty miles a day for three days—to raise money for breast cancer research.

It was amazing. I went down and waved them all in as they came. They had a ceremony; they had raised 7.6 million dollars. There were over three thousand people walking. A lot of the walkers were dressed in pink—they were cancer victors—people who had overcome it. There were even men walking with pictures of their wives who had died from breast cancer. I thought it was incredible.

There wasn't one mention about it in the major San Diego papers. I said, "Isn't that just something." We have to be an island of positive influence because all you see in the paper today is about celebrities and their bad behavior. Here you have all these thousands of people out there walking and trying to make a difference, and nobody thinks it's news.

So every morning I pump people up about what life's about, about what's going on. That's what my Chief Spiritual Officer job is about.

Wright

I had the pleasure of reading one of your releases, *The Leadership Pill*.

Blanchard

Yes.

Wright

I must admit that my first thought was how short the book was. I wondered if I was going to get my money's worth, which by the way, I most certainly did. Many of your books are brief and based on a fictitious story. Most business books in the market today are hundreds of pages in length and are read almost like a textbook.

Will you talk a little bit about why you write these short books, and about the premise of *The Leadership Pill?*

Blanchard

I really developed my relationship with Spencer Johnson when we wrote *The One Minute Manager*. As you know, he wrote, *Who Moved My Cheese*, which was a phenomenal success. He wrote children's books and is quite a storyteller.

Jesus taught by parables, which were short stories.

My favorite books are, *Jonathan Livingston Seagull* and *The Little Prince*.

Og Mandino, author of seventeen books, was the greatest of them all.

I started writing parables because people can get into the story and learn the contents of the story, and they don't bring their judgmental hats into reading. You write a regular book and they'll say, "Well, where did you get the research?" They get into that judgmental side. Our books get them emotionally involved and they learn.

The Leadership Pill is a fun story about a pharmaceutical company that thinks they have discovered the secret to leadership, and they can put the ingredients in a pill. When they announce it, the country goes crazy because everybody knows we need more effective leaders. When they release it, it outsells Viagra.

The founders of the company start selling off stock and they call them Pillionaires. But along comes this guy who calls himself "the effective manager," and he challenges them to a no-pill challenge. If they identify two non-performing groups, he'll take on one and let somebody on the pill take another one, and he guarantees he will out-perform that person by the end of the year. They agree, but of course they give him a drug test every week to make sure he's not sneaking pills on the side.

I wrote the book with Marc Muchnick, who is a young guy in his early thirties. We did a major study of what this interesting "Y" generation—the young people of today—want from leaders, and this is a secret blend that this effective manager uses. When you think about it, David, it is really powerful on terms of what people want from a leader.

Number one, they want integrity. A lot of people have talked about that in the past, but these young people will walk if they see people say one thing and do another. A lot of us walk to the bathroom and out into the halls to talk about it. But these people will quit. They don't want somebody to say something and not do it.

The second thing they want is a partnership relationship. They hate superior/subordinate. I mean, what awful terms those are. You know, the "head" of the department and the hired "hands"—you don't even give them a head. "What do you do? I'm in supervision. I see things a lot clearer than these stupid idiots." They want to be treated as partners; if they can get a financial partnership, great. If they can't, they really want a minimum of psychological partnership where they can bring their brains to work and make decisions.

Then finally, they want affirmation. They not only want to be caught doing things right, but they want to be affirmed for who they are. They want to be known as individual people, not as numbers.

So those are the three ingredients that this effective manager uses. They are wonderful values when you think about them.

Rank-order values for any organization is number one, integrity. In our company we call it ethics. It is our number one value. The number two value is partnership. In our company we call it relationships. Number three is affirmation—being affirmed as a human being. I think that ties into relationships, too. They are wonderful values that can drive behavior in a great way.

Wright

I believe most people in today's business culture would agree that success in business has everything to do with successful leadership. In *The Leadership Pill*, you present a simple but profound premise, that leadership is not something you do to people, it's something you do *with* them. At face value, that seems incredibly obvious. But you must have found in your research and observations that leaders in today's culture do not get this. Would you speak to that issue?

Blanchard

Yes. I think what often happens in this is the human ego. There are too many leaders out there who are self-serving. They're not leaders who have service in mind. They think the sheep are there for the benefit of the shepherd. All the power, money, fame, and recognition moves up the hierarchy. They forget that the real action in business is not up the hierarchy—it's in the one-to-one, moment-to-moment interactions that your frontline people have with your customers. It's how the phone is answered. It's how problems are dealt with and those kinds of things. If you don't think that you're doing leadership *with* them—rather, you're doing it to them—after a while they won't take care of your customers.

I was at a store once (not Nordstrom's, where I normally would go) and I thought of something I had to share with my wife, Margie. I asked the guy behind the counter in Men's Wear, "May I use your phone?"

He said, "No!"

"You're kidding me," I said. "I can always use the phone at Nordstrom's."

"Look, buddy," he said, "they won't let *me* use the phone here. Why should I let you use the phone?"

That is an example of leadership that's done *to* employees not *with* them. People want a partnership. People want to be involved in a way that really makes a difference.

Wright

Dr. Blanchard, the time has flown by and there are so many more questions I'd like to ask you. In closing, would you mind sharing with our readers some thoughts on success? If you were mentoring a small group of men and women, and one of their central goals was to become successful, what kind of advice would you give them?

Blanchard

Well, I would first of all say, "What are you focused on?" If you are focused on success as being, as I said earlier, accumulation of money, recognition, power, or status, I think you've got the wrong target. What you need to really be focused on is how you can be generous in the use of your time and your talent and your treasure and touch. How can you serve people rather than be served? How can you develop caring, loving relationships with people? My sense is if you will focus on those things, success in the traditional sense will come to you. But if you go out and say, "Man, I'm going to make a fortune, and I'm going to do this," and have that kind of attitude, you might get some of those numbers. I think you become an adult, however, when you realize you are here to give rather than to get. You're here to serve not to be served. I would just say to people, "Life is such a very special occasion. Don't miss it by aiming at a target that bypasses other people, because we're really here to serve each other."

Wright

Well, what an enlightening conversation, Dr. Blanchard. I really want you to know how much I appreciate all the time you've taken with me for this interview. I know that our readers will learn from this, and I really appreciate your being with us today.

Blanchard

Well, thank you so much, David. I really enjoyed my time with you. You've asked some great questions that made me think, and I hope my answers are helpful to other people because as I say, life is a special occasion.

Wright

Today we have been talking with Dr. Ken Blanchard. He is coauthor of the phenomenal best selling book, *The One Minute Manager*. The fact that he's the Chief Spiritual Officer of his company should make us all think about how we are leading our companies and leading our families and leading anything, whether it is in church or civic organizations. I know I will.

Thank you so much, Dr. Blanchard, for being with us today.

Blanchard

Good to be with you, David.

About Kenneth Blanchard...

Few people have created more of a positive impact on the day-to-day management of people and companies than Dr. Kenneth Blanchard, who is known around the world simply as "Ken."

When Ken speaks, he speaks from the heart with warmth and humor. His unique gift is to speak to an audience and communicate with each individual as if they were alone and talking one-on-one. He is a polished storyteller with a knack for making the seemingly complex easy to understand.

Ken has been a guest on a number of national television programs, including Good Morning America and The Today Show. He has been featured in Time, People, U.S. News & World Report, and a host of other popular publications.

He earned his bachelor's degree in Government and Philosophy from Cornell University, his master's degree in Sociology and Counseling from Colgate University, and his PhD in Educational Administration and Leadership from Cornell University.

Dr. Ken Blanchard
The Ken Blanchard Companies
125 State Place
Escondido, California 92029
800.728.6000
Fax: 760.489.8407
www.kenblanchard.com

Chapter Eight

An interview with...

Sherial Bratcher

David Wright (Wright)

Today we're talking with Sherial Bratcher. Sherial has a passion for bringing people together and is founder of one of Las Vegas's most successful Business Networking organizations, Diamond Star Networking Events. She is dynamic and has a gift for connecting people by combining a winning attitude with warmth, professionalism, and the ability to help others grow and make their dreams become reality. She is a contributing writer to www.vegascommunityonline.org and co-hosts a local radio program. She has received widespread recognition as an expert in the networking community with her ability to tap into local resources, fundraise, organize large galas, and connect people and businesses. Equipped with heart, intuition, and business savvy, Sherial is one of Las Vegas's premiere philanthropists. Sherial has owned several businesses, held government contracts in excess of $2 million, and developed and supported employment programs for the disabled. She is an innovative businesswoman who brings a fresh approach to business and social networking by providing an outstanding combination of imaginative, practical ways to connect people by providing extraordinary venues and excellent speakers. She partners with members to create a networking path that helps them maximize their potential. Sherial has changed the face of networking by assisting her members to shift from the ordinary to the extraordinary.

Welcome to *Blueprint for Success*, Sherial.

Wright

What is networking and why is it important?

Sherial Bratcher (Bratcher)

The "Secret" everyone is talking about is waiting for you. A gift of the secret laws of the universe that enhances life is waiting to be received! I learned this intuitively as I was trying to find employees who would hire disabled people. I was told it was too "hard" a sell, but I focused on the "positives" of how people's lives could improve. What I was doing intuitively is now "the talk of the town!" How do you become a world-class networker using principles of *The Secret?* By taking that leap into a world of possibility.

Being a world-class networker means our feelings and thoughts attract events. We need to focus on our accomplishments. Most people have "negative" thoughts, however, what do we "act" on? What do we focus on to live our dream lives? That is the "secret."

Networking is more than "showing up" at an event. Networking is one of the most important, successful means of growing your business. The three most important attributes of a successful networker are:

Attitude about yourself: Entrepreneurs are hard workers with courage, vision, and passion. Know your talents and accomplishments. Hold your head high. Exude self-confidence.

Attitude about your business: You've worked hard and have overcome many challenges! Whatever you have to offer is vital to the community. Talk about your business with pride.

Attitude about others: Be supportive of others' hard work. *Listen* to others. Active listening means hearing what is said and responding accordingly. Ask how you can help others and if you say you're going to do something, do it! This encourages others to do the same for you.

Before attending any mixer, do your homework. Have a short, interesting presentation of your business. Bring easy to read business cards. You only get one chance to make a first impression. Your appearance, handshake, and smile are part of this. Like attracts like. Smile and you will get one back.

Before attending any mixer, think about the fact that relationships are the basis of any business deal. Be open, and eager to share your story. Be eager to hear others; be eager to grow your business and help others.

Before attending any mixer, ask yourself:

1. Why have I chosen this mixer/event?
2. What does it offer me?
3. Whom do I want to meet?

Networking is the most productive, cost effective, easiest, and fun way of growing your business. You're at an event with huge potential for growth. Be, prepared. Have fun.

Wright

A lot of people are fearful about attending a networking event. What can they do to overcome this?

Bratcher

Everyone has fears—fear of failure, fear of success, fear of not being loved or appreciated, etc. If you are fearful in certain situations, you are not alone! You are simply human!

I experienced being homeless when I was a child. It was very frightening and I will never forget this. With assistance, we moved to Canada where life improved. I founded a number of businesses and became successful. After 9/11, I moved back to the United States, to Las Vegas. I knew no one, but I had something powerful—I had already experienced much fear and knew I could survive, and thrive.

Being an entrepreneur takes guts! It is the "road less traveled." Starting and building a business, takes passion, thinking "out of the box," and perseverance.

As an entrepreneur, whether you are just starting out or have been in business for awhile, everyone is nervous and scared. However, to accomplish what you already have and keep moving forward you had to believe in yourself, and your vision. When feeling fear, remember you are already courageous!

Acclaimed author, Judi Moreo, in her book, *You are More than Enough: Every Woman's Guide to Purpose, Passion, and Power,* cites me as an example of overcoming fear. Acknowledge the feeling so it doesn't control and/or determine your actions. You *can* control your emotions and change the way you think and act. Whenever a negative thought emerges, stop it and immediately change it to something positive. That is how I overcame my fear of returning to the United States. I thought about my past and how I had succeeded. Everyone has something or someone in life he or she can point to that is positive and uplifting. In a conscious way, focus on the positive. Be patient. This can take time and practice, but *can* be done. You *can* transform fear into victory.

Failure and success—most people are afraid of either or both! Failure is not to be feared; it is a good teacher, providing an opportunity to grow, re-evaluate, and feel compassion. The other side of the coin is fear of success. What could be feared about success? You might think being successful means people have certain expectations or you will need to be in the limelight or that you don't "deserve" your success. Not true! You deserve success! You worked for it. Own it, and be grateful for it.Believe in your dreams and take steps to make them happen. Nothing can take them away from you. Just believe!

Wright

I've heard that getting a mentor is a good idea. What would be the benefits of getting a mentor?

Bratcher

A mentor is an adviser, guide, teacher. This person can be a friend, colleague, relative—someone you respect and trust. A mentor can assist by offering counsel, providing a "cheering" section, constructive criticism, a fresh perspective, and "brainstorm" new solutions. Many people seek a mentor who is more experienced in a particular field, having skills you want to enhance. A mentor can assist in opening new doors, helping to advance your career, or assisting you in going in new directions.

Whether you've been in business twenty years or if you are just starting out, a mentor can be invaluable. A mentor can help you assess your strengths and weaknesses, help plan short- and long-term goals, and seize new opportunities. You can have several mentors or just one. You want someone you trust, who has *your* interests at heart. A mentor can sometimes help you cope with known and unknown internal "demons" that block your success.

In seeking a mentor, look for someone who can help you develop more self-awareness and confidence, and even refer you to some movers and shakers in your area. You want a mentor who is positive, yet realistic; honest, but not brutal; self-confident, but not arrogant. Seek someone who wants to assist you to be your most authentic self. Discuss what you can offer the mentor. Seek mentors you might want to model yourself after.

I have always had a mentor. My first mentor lives his dream as an internationally acclaimed professional speaker and best-selling author whose books inspire positive change. I chose him because he is all I wanted to become.

A mentor can help you sidestep the "expensive" way to learn things by pointing out potential pitfalls and errors that you aren't aware of. Excellent mentors are those who listen and "coach" rather than tell you what to do.

Be clear about your goals in selecting a mentor. Is your goal to expand your business? Do you need better communication skills? Do you need help quieting those internal, negative "demons"? Be realistic about your expectations. A mentor can take you just so far—the real work is up to you!

A mentor can be right in front of you—a friend, colleague, or someone you met at a networking event. Don't be shy! Most people are flattered to be asked. Offer to take this person to lunch or coffee to talk about this. Mentoring can be long-term or a few conversations. You both want clarify what kind of a commitment you can arrange and what you can contribute to the relationship. Let your mentor(s) know you are grateful for assistance. Show this by being respectful of your mentor's time and effort; let him or her see you are putting in the effort to apply what you've learned. Show your appreciation—a handwritten thank-you note, a special lunch, etc.

To seek help or counsel does *not* make you weak, stupid, or incompetent—quite the contrary. To seek advice and counsel means you are intelligent enough to want to improve yourself, strong enough to have the guts to do it, and competent enough to find the right person. Also, many schools, universities, Small Business Associations, and trade organizations have mentoring programs.

Wright

How do I get people to remember who I am?

Bratcher

You've attended a networking event, collected lots of cards, had interesting conversations, and "connected" with some people. You'll follow up with them, but will others follow up with you and know who you are? If people don't remember you, they probably won't refer you or be interested in building a relationship. Being memorable is extremely important.

The first step to being memorable is knowing who you are. If *you* don't think you're memorable, why would anyone else? Know who you are and how special you are without arrogance. Have self-confidence oozing out of you—self-confidence that draws people in. *That's* memorable.

You must honestly assess yourself—strengths and weaknesses. Learn to turn your weaknesses into strengths and your strengths into greater power. Write down your strengths and everything wonderful and unique about yourself.

Everyone can do what we are all ultimately here to do, and that is to be the best "me" that I can be. I *can* be the best Sherial Bratcher that I can be. Being authentic and our best "self," gives others that space as well. Being memorable begins from the inside out. Put your list somewhere so you see it every day. Every morning, smile at yourself in the mirror—a big, genuine smile. Begin every day on a positive note.

Now, what can you outwardly do to be that memorable person you already are? Impeccable grooming is a must. That alone makes you memorable. Impeccable grooming means you're clean, you smell good, your breath is fresh, and your clothing is pressed and well fitted. Impeccable grooming means you are a savvy professional. Wear something distinctive and classy. Know your style. Enhance your good points. Don't be outrageous, but don't just blend in with everyone else.

Whatever you do, be present to the here and now. You are dealing with intelligent, hard-working people. They can tell if you're not listening carefully, or responding appropriately. At a networking event, ask thought-provoking questions. Ask people their "story," what they love about what they do, how they got started, etc. Focus on the other person and on him or her alone. By giving people your full attention, you will make them feel special—and they will remember you.

When you are telling people about yourself, keep it simple. Your name, company name, and service or product is easy to remember. Tell a short story about yourself. People remember stories.

Make your business card easy to read, especially your contact information. People don't have time and magnifying glasses to see tiny print and go through an overly busy business card. A simple, creative easy to read card provides more incentive to read it and potentially use your service and/or refer you. Also, have a stack of inexpensive, attractive blank cards handy. Sending a handwritten note that you enjoyed conversing with someone is a lost art. With so few people doing that these days, you are sure to be remembered. You can actually make someone's day with that "little" gesture of consideration.

Keep in mind *you* are your business. *You* are your best advertisement. How you interact with people is representative of your business. Think and act positively during every interaction. Be grounded in the gratitude that you woke up to another day, and you have wonderful talents and gifts to offer others. You also appreciate and value others for being themselves. Every day is opportunity to be more memorable, more true to yourself, and contribute something valuable to the world. Whatever your business, everyone is interconnected and invaluable to each other. With that philosophy, you are unstoppable, valued, and will always be memorable.

Wright

What is "Personal Branding" and why is it so important?

Bratcher

Ever notice the label on your jeans or t-shirt? What makes you buy one product over another? The *brand!* I buy such-and-such soap, or such-and-such computers. It's about *branding.* Think of corporations that have serious name recognition like Nike or Wal-Mart. That's what you want—name recognition. The way to do that is to brand *yourself. You* are your business and you want people to instantly recognize you. Whether you are just starting out or have been in business ten years, it's never too late or too early to brand yourself. *You* are your brand.

A personal brand is a vibrant, compelling tool of self-promotion. Another exciting aspect of branding is the opportunity to explore who you are, gain insight into your core values, and assist you in finding your authentic self. It helps you learn and expand what makes you unique and is an invaluable tool for inner growth. Branding also assists in cultivating your image, increasing visibility, and generating excitement and interest in you.

In this Internet and e-mail age, personal branding has become even more important. For many, their first introduction and/or impression of you is your Web site or an e-mail they receive from you. This is where personal branding can make the difference between a new client/customer or not. What makes you continually go to a site or eager to open a particular e-mail? The brand, name recognition, trust. You know that this is a person and/or a business you can rely on and recommend.

Personal branding is the process where people and businesses are marketed as brands and success comes from self-packaging. A personal brand usually has four main elements: personality, appearance, competencies, and differentiation. These elements provide your core message and provide the main components of your "pitch." As you think about these four elements, the most important part is the "foundation." *The foundation is being your authentic self and the benefits people receive from you that they don't receive from anyone else or any other business.*

Now it's time to examine the four basics, balancing being realistic with "bragging" about yourself. You want to brand yourself as someone who has some specific advantage to offer and to also create a positive feeling about you.

What is it about your personality and characteristics that are special, and make people want to do business with you? Write at least ten characteristics that make you stand out. Be authentic. If you know you're shy, write about your incredible ability to listen. If it takes you time to warm up to people, write about your ability to be objective. Talk to trusted friends and/or colleagues. Getting honest feedback from people you trust can be of great assistance.

Examine every aspect of your appearance, your personal look, your Web site, business cards, brochures, etc. Look around your place of business. Is everything clean, neat, and unique to you? Are your marketing materials creative? Do they tell your story in an exciting, distinctive, and interesting way that grabs people's attention? Be your own worst critic and best advocate. Don't be afraid to "re-invent" yourself.

Doing this self-branding might be a good time to do a full scale or partial makeover, especially if your business is not reaching the level of success you would like. You want to strive to constantly improve who you are and what you do.

Speaking of competencies, what do you do better than anyone else? What would make people come back again? Taking additional classes, attending seminars, doing research of the newest aspects in your field could increase your competencies. Another area that shouldn't be neglected is doing some volunteer work, offering to teach a class, or, being a speaker on a panel. This creates more visibility, increases your skills, and indicates your interest in your community.

What differentiates you from others? What are your greatest strengths? Are you a great problem-solver? Do you give the fastest and best service? Uncompromising focus on what you do is what adds value to others. You are constantly cultivating your image with everything you do. I use a car mechanic because he gives great service and is extremely kind. He takes care of people's cars—even people who can't pay all at once. He's a man with heart. That makes him distinctive.

Remember, you are your own Public Relations person. You are a leader because of your excellence and commitment to yourself and others.

Wright

What is the Best Way for me to get and give referrals?

Bratcher

The first step in learning to get and give referrals is to be courteous and grateful. While most professionals use the word "referral," other options are "recommending" and "introducing." They give a more personal feeling, and yet maintain a sense of professionalism.

Receiving a referral is an honor and should be treated as such. Getting a referral means that someone believes in you, and is an acknowledgement of their trust. Sounds easy? Basic? Everybody knows this. *Not true!* Everyone *doesn't* know this. There are many people who need referrals, but don't get them. One of the most important keys to gaining referrals is how you treat your established clients or customers. How you handle your *present* clients or customers reflects on how your *future* may take shape. Keeping established clients is crucial to getting new ones.

When attending networking events, take some deep breaths and focus. Put everything else out of your mind other than the person in front of you. Make eye contact with everyone you meet, shake hands, and repeat their name, saying, "Hello Joe." Ask about him or her and their business. This lets people know this is about them not *you*—your turn will come later.

Most important of all: Listen. Don't interrupt anyone. Wait a few seconds after it appears the other person is finished and gather your thoughts. Don't rush as though you want to give your "spiel" and move on. There is nothing more important than the person you are with at that moment. Don't be the person who is giving your card to people you don't know, talking nonstop, and not listening to anyone else. Most people get rid of those cards. Ask people for their business card. There's always someone you meet at a networking event you can refer to someone else. What you give comes back tenfold. This will also enhance the chances of people wanting to refer you.

Carry some clients' business cards and let them know you will give out their card to others. By doing this, you are actively indicating your interest in helping others build their business. This will, in turn, encourage them to do the same for you.

Spend some "quiet time" thinking about which people in your target market you would like to get referrals from. Think *big!* Aim for the movers and shakers. The best way to get a referral from them is to refer others to them. Responsible professionals know that referrals and word-of-mouth can make or break a business or relationship. When you make a referral, let others know you are sending people their way. Let them know they can expect to hear from so-and-so. Know that other people's success is yours also. Let others know that's what you believe and show it by making referrals. This also opens the door to ask others to make referrals to you.

Sometimes when I am at a social event and I am out of cards, I even write down someone's information on a napkin indicating my interest in him or her. A warm handshake, warm smile, eye contact, and mentioning something you might have in common go a long way in establishing a connection. If you offer a referral or get a referral, again, immediately follow up. Whether an established client or someone you meet at a networking event gives you a referral, send a personalized thank-you note, phone call, or e-mail indicating your appreciation.

You are already becoming the king or queen of referrals.

Wright

What is so important about following up and how do I follow up after meeting people?

Bratcher

You attended a mixer, met some new people, and exchanged business cards. If you're hoping your phone will ring off the hook, you'll get tons of e-mails, or people will be knocking on your door, you might have to sit there and just wait. Attending mixers, and getting and giving business cards are only the beginning. "The Art of the Follow-Up" is your next step up the ladder of success and doorway to your dreams.

The first step in learning this art is to have a plan and goal in mind. For most us, the goal is usually the same—building and expanding our business, forming mutually beneficial relationships, and developing an excellent reputation.

An important aspect of planning is deciding which method of contact to initiate. The goals and the plans may vary, but it is important to keep both in mind. Following up should not be random. Whether it's a note, e-mail, or phone call, have a plan, and a goal. You are building bridges and forming partnerships. This is exciting, essential, and even *fun!*

One thing that works really well is if I get home with a stack of business cards, I go through the cards and jot down on the back of the card something I remember about the person. I do that right away so I don't forget who is who. The next day, I prioritize who I want to contact first. Who did I "connect" with the most? Whose business blends the best with mine? Who can I assist? Who appeared to be the movers and shakers? These are the people to contact first. After that, I move through the rest of the cards and prioritize them (i.e., who to contact in a week or three weeks). Again, follow-up is not random; being organized helps achieve the desired results. Creating a "Follow-up Tickler File" is a must so I know who and how I contacted each person and what each response was. This tickler file is part of my day and essential to building business and developing relationships.

The day after attending a mixer I usually send a thank-you note and follow up with an e-mail or phone call three or four days later, especially to the first group of people I want to reconnect with. People love to receive mail, especially a handwritten note, and it's even more enjoyable if you mention something about your conversation. This will make you memorable, indicate your interest, your attention to detail, and your ability to handle yourself professionally and courteously. If you send a note, be sure to include your business card. If you call, be sure to leave your phone number at the beginning and end of the message. Have a smile on your face when you do. You want to sound cheerful, friendly, and *not* scripted. If you leave a message, put the person's name in your tickler file to follow up again in a couple of days. If you get the person on the phone, remind him or her of what you talked about at the mixer. Ask about something the person mentioned so he or she knows you were paying attention. You might want to suggest a cup of coffee, lunch, or someone the person might want to meet (always remember that you have contacts that can be of interest to others). If your initial contact is by e-mail, do the same thing. Create an interesting subject so it stands out. However, do not use all caps—that looks like spam.

No matter how you initiate the follow-up contact, do your research. Check your notes on the back of the person's business card. Whether you have written a note on the card or not, go to the person's Web site. Learn what you can about the person and his or her business. If the person has a bio, look at that and see if there is anything that helps you remember something about the person or something you might have in common. Being prepared is extremely important. The person might actually call or e-mail you right back.

Even if you don't get a response from someone, still keep the person's name in your tickler file. Approximately every six weeks, send an e-mail with an update about what you are doing and a reminder of who you are. Keep it short and simple, but keep your name in front of the person. It's only a matter of time and he or she will want to do business or refer you to someone else.

Another method of following up is that when I receive an e-mail from an organization or person with a question, I do something called "Instant Turnaround." The exact moment I finish reading the e-mail, I obtain the person's phone number. I do anything I can to get a phone number within the next two minutes. Then I call the person right back and say something like, "Hi, this is Sherial Bratcher. I was in the office when your e-mail came through and I thought I'd call you back!" I say this with a big smile on my face. *People love this.* I have never done this without completely blowing the caller away and getting great responses.

Follow-up, done correctly and consistently, is a catalyst for success and opens new pathways to business and social relationships. As with any other art or skill, practice makes perfect. The more you do it, the better and more comfortable you'll get doing it and the rewards are potentially unlimited.

Wright

Cold calling can be a valuable tool for people, but it gets a lot of people nervous. What suggestions do you have on how to make cold calling easier and more doable for people?

Bratcher

When most people think of "cold-calling," they break into a sweat. Most people fear rejection, the phone feels like it weighs a ton and everything they know flies out the window. Many people may not have "done their homework." They may not be clear on the benefits of cold calling and are not properly prepared. Cold calling is not for the faint of heart, but entrepreneurs are anything but that. To be an entrepreneur one has already shown courage, vision, perseverance, and the ability to be extraordinary.

Cold calling is *not* a battle. It is a method of advertising and, if done correctly, can substantially expand your business. Cold calling can identify and attract potential prospects and generate leads. A great part of success with cold calling is your attitude about yourself, your service, and your attitude about cold calling. The phone is not an albatross around your neck, but can be your best friend—as long as you do your homework.

What do I mean by "homework?" The first part of the homework is to think about how you or your product or service can benefit others. Write a list of the benefits of your products or services including the benefits of working with *you*. Write what makes you unique and how you bring added value to a prospect. Writing this list builds confidence and can be used as the outline of your "presentation." Another way of turning a "cold" call "lukewarm" is to send out information in advance. Even if the prospect hasn't seen or read it, you've opened the door.

The next bit of homework is to write and re-write the presentation, until it's part of you. Read it to a trusted friend. Ask for feedback. It's better to hear criticism from a friend than to hear some not so constructive criticism from a prospective client. The presentation should be concise, informative, and immediately grab people's attention. Identify yourself, your company, and explain that you are following up on the information you sent. Give a brief overview of your company, personalizing as much as possible by mentioning some information you have researched about their company.

You don't want to sound as though you're reading a script. Once you have the prospect on the line, there is no second chance to make a first impression and the first impression only takes a few seconds. In the first sixty seconds of the call, you will need to get the prospect's mind away from whatever he or she was doing and generate enough interest so the prospect will stay on the line. Don't ask if this is a good time to talk. Most people will say no. Rather, if the person sounds busy, tell him or her so and ask when would be a better time to talk. Give the person a couple of options to pin down a time and date. You might be asked why you're calling. This will give you the perfect opening to deliver your attention-grabbing introduction.

Remember, research first. Learn everything you can about the person and company you are calling. This builds confidence. The more you know about the person you are calling, the more you can be seen as a trusted advisor rather than another annoying sales pitch.

This brings us to "pitch." You want to establish rapport. Listen to the person's tone of voice and the pace in which he or she is speaking. Match what you hear! This is key! Most of us want to talk to people like ourselves.

Give the prospect a chance to ask questions and don't be shy about asking questions. Find out what people need, where they and/or their businesses are in "pain" and be prepared to tell them how you can help. This is a conversation, not a monologue. Listen attentively and without interruption. You learn a lot from active listening. . The more people talk, the more interest they are indicating. Once you have established rapport and interest, move into setting up an appointment. Again, give a choice between two dates. After the phone call, immediately follow up with a thank-you e-mail for taking the time to talk with you and confirm your appointment. Briefly go over the pain and how only you can alleviate it.

What most people consider the *real* challenge is getting past the "gatekeeper." A lot of literature about this was written before voicemail. Many organizations rely on voicemail, using it as their primary and sometimes exclusive screening mechanism. Since you've already done your homework, you can leave a message because you know two or three of your prospective clients' major needs and your ability to solve the person's problems. Speak clearly, giving your phone number in the beginning and end of your message. Sound friendly, professional, and excited about what you can do for your prospective client.

Now you've potentially sent some brochures, but either way, you *have* done your homework. You've made a contact, but the last, most important work is yet to be done: Again, follow up, probably with an e-mail. You don't want to be a pest, but you know you can help your prospective client and that you are the best person for the job. Remind the person of this. Give your prospect a few days and call back to make sure your e-mail was received. Remind the person about what you can do for him or her. If there was anything that created a "spark" between the two of you during your conversation, you want to focus on that.

Close the deal. You can do it! Your next sale is only one call away!

Wright

I've heard that doing some kind of philanthropy is a good idea. Do you think that's true?

Bratcher

My experience in giving back to my community is one of the most rewarding aspects of my life. Early in my career and for many years, I worked to find employment for disabled people. Since coming to Las Vegas, I have hosted several charitable galas. Giving back to the community fills me with joy and builds new relationships. This has been a big component of my success and is what networking is about—connecting, being part of a community, and sharing our skills, hearts, and good fortune with others.

Everyone knows someone who is struggling with some issue. At some time in everyone's life, compassion and generosity has made the difference between life and death, being homeless, or provided help to find a cure for a disease. For many professionals, the bulk of their business comes from within the community in which they live. What better way to build a distinctive and respected reputation than to find some way to help the very people who contribute to your livelihood?

Another aspect of being philanthropic is its "transformative" quality. This "transformation" begins with a vision for change. Who are more visionary than entrepreneurs? Whether it's Sam Walton, Henry Ford, or the garage owner who had a vision of fixing people's cars combined with kindness and compassion, what they have in common is the vision of something better than before. One need only look around to see how much need there is for "change" if we have the eyes, heart, and courage to see it and the vision to be change agents. Entrepreneurs are naturally change agents. Even if you work for a company, you are still an entrepreneur because *you* are always your own business. Entrepreneurs are innovators, "out of the box" thinkers, and doers—extraordinary by every standard.

Most entrepreneurs have a vision to be and do something unusual. They are original thinkers who are creating change every day. They are highly motivated opinion-makers and leaders who create new paradigms, open boundaries, and have the potential to alleviate suffering and enhance others' lives. Like a stone cast into the water creating ripples, every act of kindness and compassion reverberates throughout.

Business and social networking builds a sense of community. No business is too small, no contribution too little, no time volunteered too insignificant to make a difference. The "transformative" quality of philanthropy is also a two-way street. Each act of kindness is a catalyst for internal growth in a positive way. When a person donates to a charity, serves at a food kitchen, or hosts a gala, he or she has the potential of finding within a depth of compassion, and a heart that unconditionally loves. Philanthropy can be a doorway to self-development and builds trust and loyalty in our community.

People know the charity events I host, and I've built a reputation as someone who donates to charities; but the rewards go far beyond any event. When I close my eyes at night, I know that someone else might be a little better off because of the work others who work with me have done. They and I have been catalysts for change; maybe we have even been an inspiration. I am always inspired by others' acts of kindness and benevolence.

Look at your own life and those times you couldn't have "made it" without the help of others. I would never have accomplished what I have without the help, kindness, and philanthropy of others.

If life and creating a vibrant, growing business, cultivating business and social relationships isn't also about philanthropy, it is a lost opportunity personally and professionally, and a loss to the community. Be a change agent. The time is now. The opportunity is *always*.

About Sherial Bratcher...

SHERIAL BRATCHER has a passion for bringing people together and is founder of one of Las Vegas's most successful business networking organizations, DiamondStarNetworkingEvents. She is dynamic and has a gift for connecting people by combining a winning attitude with warmth, professionalism, and the ability to help others grow and make their dreams become reality. She is a contributing writer to www.Lasvegasnetworking.org and co-hosts a local radio program. She has received widespread recognition as an expert in the networking community with her ability to tap into local resources, fundraise, organize large galas, and connect people and businesses. Equipped with heart, intuition, and business savvy, Sherial is one of Las Vegas's premiere philanthropists. Sherial has owned several businesses, held government contracts in excess of $1 million, and developed and supported employment programs for the disabled. She is an innovative businesswoman who brings a fresh approach to business and social networking by providing an outstanding combination of imaginative, practical ways to connect people by providing extraordinary venues and excellent speakers. She partners with members to create a networking path that helps them maximize their potential. Sherial has changed the face of networking by assisting her members to shift from the ordinary to the extraordinary.

Sherial Bratcher, Founder/CEO
DiamondStarNetworkingEvents
4680 S. Polaris Suite 250
Las Vegas, NV 89103
702.248.3568 (office)
702.285.8984 (cell)
www.diamondstarnetworkingevents.com

Chapter Nine

An *interview with…*

Deborah George-Feres

David Wright (Wright)

Today we're talking with Deborah George-Feres. I would like to introduce her by giving some of her thoughts. She says, "If I had a dollar for every time someone has said, 'I should have listened to my gut feelings, I would be a wealthy woman today!' Many people do not acknowledge their intuition as a credible source of information, they usually ignore this remarkable tool because most are programmed to rely on other methods of information for their decision-making, problem-solving, planning, organizing, and facilitating their road to success. As a result, they are often stymied in many of these areas because they lack access to timely and accurate information that will move them in a positive direction." Deborah defines intuition as "insight into one's inner wisdom and higher spirit. Someone once said intuition is an inner knowing about an undeniable truth or information your conscious and logical mind wouldn't normally know. It differs from common sense, which relies on someone's philosophy or personal perspective rather than a strong feeling about the right path."

She says, "I strongly believe intuition can lead a person to success and that no one knows better than an individual what success is. However, society provides us with a standard definition that many of us use as a barometer to measure how close we are to achieving it. The standard usually comes in three main categories: wealth, fame, and educational achievement. Most successful people fall into the wealth or fame category, and usually demonstrate and enjoy their success through material possessions. But many others are somewhere in between and are constantly trying to rise to the standard. It's unfortunate, but over the years, I've seen a slight shift in attitudes towards educational achievement. My sense is that wealth and fame is more highly desired.

"Instead of working from society's standard definition of success, the use of your intuition can provide you with your quintessential definition and lead you to your own personal success. Intuition is a key ingredient in the pot of success because it provides clear guidance that encourages growth."

Deborah, welcome to *Blueprint for Success!*

Deborah George-Feres (George-Feres)

Thank you, I am happy to be here, David.

Wright

In your introduction you mentioned that most people's ideas of success fall within three categories. We know, however, that there are many other definitions of success and that it is largely dependent on the individual. What is your definition of success? And what do you say to someone who seeks success based on the three categories and has yet to achieve it?

George-Feres

My definition of success is very simple. I define it as a lifetime process of growing, sharing, learning, and a progressive movement forward. It's really about finding your bliss and following it to a productive path. A very good definition I discovered recently reads: *"Success is defined as 'the progressive realization of a worthwhile goal.' If you are doing the things that are moving you toward the attainment of your goal, then you are 'successful' even if you are not there yet."*

Society usually measures success on an individual's personal accomplishments. I measure my success on what I've helped others to accomplish, a more fulfilling measurement for me. For people who seek one of the three categories, I would encourage them to first examine their intentions. You must understand your true motives. Do you want to be successful for the greater good, such as through philanthropic work, or influencing public policy to change the social and economic landscape of the disenfranchised, or is it your desire to fulfill your dreams? Whatever your reasons, you must be clear about them. If you haven't received clarity, what you may discover on the road to your success might be a very big surprise or even disappointment.

I would like to follow up on this point with a personal story. Some years ago, I was a sophomore in college. During that time, many of my friends were very driven in pursuing their dreams. Although, some were clearer and more focused than others, most knew the path they wanted to take. This wasn't true for one of my closest friends who were very unsure about his future. Although, he worked extremely hard to be an exceptional student, his drive and determination came from the need to gain his father's approval. Don't get me wrong, we all want our parent's acceptance, it's part of our innate nature to please them. However, his desire was to achieve the same kind of notoriety his father had gained. You see, his father was a highly successful medical doctor. Needless to say, he became very unhappy and realized that being a doctor wasn't his true passion, though it was what his father wanted for him. Later, he dropped out of college to pursue his interest in the culinary arts.

I used this story to illustrate how important it is to be clear about your reasons for achieving success. Had my friend examined his intentions, he would have followed his aspirations sooner. Isn't it unfortunate that some people desire success purely because they want what others have and would do just about anything to gain it? I'm afraid that if your desires don't originate from your authentic self, the outcome may result in a lost opportunity to live the life that is right for you.

Understanding your intentions will help you to effectively utilize your experience and expertise to create your philosophy of life. This philosophy will clarify your personal mission and guide you to your personal success. The best advice I can give to a person who seeks out the traditional types of success is to trust, use, and rely on their intuition for guidance. This heightened sense can lead them to their right path.

To summarize, utilizing your intuition can produce an idea that is remarkably different from the other ideas that have been used over and over again, but packaged differently. Please don't misunderstand me; there isn't anything wrong with repeating great ideas. Many people find success doing so. But, what if you can produce something remarkably new, gain the success you seek, and achieve pioneer status all at the same time? I think most people would prefer the latter and your intuition can be the tool to make extraordinary things happen.

Wright

How do you know when you are on the path to success, and how do you know what you need to be successful?

George-Feres

You know when you're on the path to success when there's progress. Basically, the path produces growth; maybe the growth is incremental, nevertheless, there's growth and that growth keeps propelling you into the direction that brings more prosperity or moves you closer to your goals. And sometimes even more difficulties. Fredrick Douglas once said that no progress happens without struggles. If progress is slow, it doesn't mean that things are not happening. You may be in a different season, which may be the planting season. The planting season is a time for sowing seeds, fertilizing crops, and waiting for the harvest. You can apply this analogy to success in that a great part of it requires patience. Patience is very essential in establishing a successful path.

You may say, "Well, Deborah, that isn't necessarily true because there are so many people who, after they have ventured out, have achieved immediate success. So what is it that makes them successful so quickly?" That's a good question because I often see it—I know people who say, "I'm going to do it," and they do it and achieved immediate success. I believe that they are either using a combination of luck mixed with perfect timing and the right resources (whether human or capital), or they have a secret that they are unwilling to share. But for most of us, we are missing one or all of these elements at any given time, so our success comes at a slower rate.

Because we live in a quick-fix society, it isn't surprising that most of us want to get there quickly. But there is a reason why the proverb "Patience is a virtue" is important. Although it can be very difficult, patience allows you to establish a solid foundation. It prepares you for the things you'll encounter along the way and will keep you steadfast once you're there. For people who seek immediate success, I urge them to integrate patience into their success strategy.

A simple thought about patience is to remember how you have developed from infancy to adulthood. The important fact is that it didn't just happen at once, it happened over time. So the same is true when you're on the path to success. Success can be a long arduous road. At times, you may get discourage and feel as though you'll never get there. It's sad to say, but some never do because the path they are on has them spinning their wheels.

Having an attuned sense of intuition can positively influence your chances of success because it recognizes emerging opportunities and makes accurate assessments of your needs. Accessing your intuition can keep you from making the same choices or doing the same things that have produced ineffective results. Your intuition can take you off a path that has derailed your success and put you on the right track. So what you need to be successful is intuition coupled with perseverance and a sustained commitment to your goals. This goes back to what I mentioned before about success being relative. I strongly believe that the definition of success varies with each individual. Your intuition is a useful tool to assist you with that definition. Having your personal definition helps you to be explicitly clear about your direction. This concept of using intuition to achieve success is so fascinating because it implies that success comes from knowing, understanding, and utilizing what's within, and how wonderful is that?

Wright

What do you think are the biggest obstacles people face in trying to become successful?

George-Feres

The biggest obstacles are limited resources and fear. Of those two, fear is perhaps the most prominent—fear of success, failure, taking risks, competition, etc. Fear is a defense mechanism. It warns us of danger. Sometimes the danger is real, sometimes it is perceived. Fear reminds us of our immortality and sometimes provides us with the proper mechanisms to protect ourselves or those we love. This complex emotion is often difficult to comprehend; but this emotion is a valuable tool once you can manage it. It can serve as a resource for you just like your intuition or anything else you rely on for guidance. Even though there are benefits of fear, some fears inhibit your ability to move forward.

Let's examine fear of competition, which is very common among many business leaders and entrepreneurs. As a businesswoman I am constantly thinking about my competitors in terms of how I can acquire a sustained competitive advantage. Thus, it is very likely that if a new entrepreneur enters into an industry that is overcrowded or is growing exponentially, the first thing they will think about is competition and how they can gain a competitive advantage. And they should do so because it's a wise business strategy. Although we all benefit from healthy competition from time to time, for some it can be very intimidating. In my opinion, fear of competition is a sign of weakness; it indicates that you do not have confidence in yourself, your products, or services. Also, fear of competition may inhibit your progress because it might keep you from venturing out into new territory.

To effectively manage your fear of competition, you should develop the right perspective about it. For example, competition can be an opportunity for growth. It is a way for you to set yourself apart from your competitors. You can do this by developing your differentiation strategy, defined as a set of actions designed to produce a non-standardized way of delivering products, goods, or services that customers view as uniquely different and serve as an added value to them.

In today's competitive market this strategy is important because it can neutralize competition and help you increase market share. In developing your differentiation strategy, there are four strategic questions you must address:

1. Who are your competitors and what percentage of the market do they share?

2. How can you reinvent, expand, or diversify your product line and/or improve on services?

3. What is the distinct difference and value of your products and/or services?

4. What is your sustained competitive advantage and how can you turn that into an added value for your consumers?

Once you have addressed these questions effectively, you really can begin to place competition in its proper context.

Earlier I briefly touched on the concept of fear of success and failure, so I would like to provide more details about them. Fear of success is an interesting concept because if you think about it, why should anyone be afraid of success? Well, some people are afraid of succeeding because maybe they feel that they won't be able to manage success once they've achieved it. Some even adhere to the belief that people only rise to their highest level of incompetence. Believe me, I've heard that many, many times.

For some of us, being successful means that there's more responsibility, which can be very scary. For example, the responsibility for a larger business venture equates to greater opportunity for failure. Fear of failure is actually very similar and often tied to fear of success. The one difference is that failure affects our ego and pride. Also, most of us are taught that we only have one chance for success and are programmed to believe that we cannot rebound from a bad business decision or traumatic life experience; that simply isn't true. There are amazing stories of people who are reinventing their lives every day by turning their failures into successes.

The reason I spent so much time discussing fear as the biggest obstacle is because it is as natural to us as any other strong emotion. Every intelligent living creature, animal or human, shares this emotion. Steering clear of your fears may cause you to unconsciously self-sabotage by giving up far too early in the process or allowing others to influence you to give up.

Wright

What are the key elements for success?

George-Feres

There are many elements of success, but the fundamental elements are creativity, courage, integrity, intuition, and relationships. These are key elements because they position you to obtain sound, practical advice, communicate effectively, display imaginative thinking, maintain self-control, be credible, and effectively deal with transition or change.

Let's explore courage and creativity more in depth. Many of society's remarkable inventions were brought into existence by individuals with creative minds. Creativity is used by some doctors to help injured patients heal. It is the one activity that anyone can do regardless of his or her talents, expertise, or skills. So if doctors can use it to help stimulate healing in their patients, why can't you use it to achieve success? Unfortunately, for many of us, our creativity is stifled because we were programmed to utilize more tangible sources of information and are encouraged to seek out the road most often taken. It is time to awaken the creative side of our brain and use it to our benefit. Your creativity can lead you to develop new approaches for your business or it can lead you to do something different in your life.

Above all the key elements of success, courage is the most important one because courage requires action. Taking action will increase your chances of success exponentially. This action should be primarily proactive. Courage means that there is action irrespective of fear or apprehension. It may require you to make a decision to launch a new product despite the risks involved or challenge a conventional thought on how something should be done. When you use your intuition, courage is accompanied by a comfortable certainty that makes it easier to take action.

Lastly, if you were to commission a research study on common traits of the most successful leaders of our time, I'm certain that along with intuitive abilities, courage would be at the top of the list.

Wright

Why do you think that intuition is such a critical element for effective leadership and successful business practice?

George-Feres

Intuition is a critical element for effective leadership and successful business practice because it enables you to make intuitive determinations before forming opinions, making judgments or decisions, and weighing alternative courses of action.

A survey conducted in May 2002 by executive search firm Christian & Timbers reveals that 45 percent of corporate executives now rely more on instinct than on facts and figures in running their businesses. In an interview with Masaru Ibuka, late Founder of Japan's Sony Corp, he was asked, "What is the secret of your success?" He responded by describing a ritual. Preceding a business decision, he would drink herbal tea and asked himself, "Should I make this deal or not?" If the tea gave him indigestion, he wouldn't make the deal. (This gives a new meaning to the phrase "gut feeling.") He said, "I trust my gut, and I know how it works. My mind is not that smart, but my body is." If not for Mr. Ibuka's philosophy and principles, would Sony have the resources and notoriety that it has today?

Intuition provides valuable information about how to connect, interact, and build relationships with others by sending out signals that show when to move forward, when to use caution, and when to stop. In today's chaotic, complex business world there exist many challenges some being limited resources such as time and money. As leaders you are often forced to make critical decisions in a hurry and without the right information. If reliable information is absent from your decision-making process, the outcome may be costly to your business and may affect employees' morale causing a decline in productivity. Therefore, knowing what decision to make and when to make it requires the right kind of information at the right time.

From a total system perspective, intuition is an effective, decision-making tool and leadership attribute because it synthesizes information from both your internal and external sources. Also, it provides innovative insights and direct knowledge that is timely and accurate. This provides for more effective decisions, assist with identifying trends in the current market, and demonstrate how to stay ahead of the competition. Cultivating and utilizing your intuition is more than just a good idea— it makes absolute business sense.

Wright

What are the strategies for harnessing intuition?

George-Feres

There are some very basic strategies that I use for harnessing intuition. In my life coaching practice, I developed a series of strategies and techniques called the Harness Intuition Program (HIP) that teaches people awareness, identification, utilization, and application of their intuition. I help them to heighten their intuitive abilities and quiet their logical mind to receive innovative insights about any situation. The strategies are very simple for anyone, and you can apply them to your life. The first set of strategies encompasses exercises and activities such as meditation, deciphering dreams, and journaling to help you increase awareness of your intuition.

Second, you learn how to identify your type of intuition, whether it is emotional, mental, or kinesthetic; most people have a combination of the three. Knowing your type of intuition helps you to clearly distinguish its messages from other culprits such fear, negative emotions, anxiety, etc., and gain mental clarity. To help the intuitive messages get through, you need to be aware of your habits, tendencies, or traits. This helps you to differentiate between your intuition and your culprits. These culprits will try to lead you astray, so you must know how your intuition communicates. Developing your intuitive ability will help eliminate these culprits along the way and strengthen your intuitive muscle. A client once asked me, how do you know when it is your intuition and not your usual culprits? I told him *you know without knowing how you know.*

Once you have identified how intuition communicates, you are ready to move to the final step, which is utilization of your intuition. This is the stage where you are using your intuition in every aspect of your life. The more you use your intuition, the stronger it becomes.

The HIP is a three-step process that is easy to apply and doesn't require any specific skill sets. All it requires is a belief in this principle and a positive attitude.

Wright

Why do you think people ignore their intuition as a credible resource?

George-Feres

People often ignore their intuition because they are programmed to do so, coupled with the fact that they really don't know it's their intuition, they may regard it as something else. Society encourages us to search for more tangible information such as data, trends, and research. It encourages us to use logic and analytical thinking, as well as other tangible sources for understanding our world and making major decisions. From early on in our development we are programmed with these concepts, and the programming continues throughout our entire lives—that's if we don't step outside of the box and seek out alternative concepts.

Thankfully, the topic of intuition has been positively featured in many major media outlets, notably in *Forbes* magazine and the *Chicago Tribune* as sources that can be trusted for big decisions. Current research validates intuition as a credible resource. According to the *Harvard Business Review,* "one decision-making tool—human intuition—seems to offer a reliable alternative to painstaking fact gathering and analysis."

However, we still have a long way to go because most of this programming happens in our educational institutions from an early age and carries through into our adult learning experience. I know from experience that our educational institutions don't support the use of intuition in the academic arena. As a college student I was only able to write papers backed by research and data. I'm certain that the same is true for students today and that it would be unacceptable if a student wrote a paper purely supported by their intuitive messages. This perspective is very limiting and it stifles not only our intuitive ability, but our creativity as well. Once you've been indoctrinated in such a rigid structure, you are more likely to ignore the hunches you receive—not because you want to, but you are trained to. However, the good news is that you can begin reprogramming your mind by applying the strategies and techniques of the Harnessing Intuition Program outlined above. To ignore intuition is a total disregard of your inner wisdom.

Wright

Are there levels of success? And if so, what are they?

George-Feres

There are varying degrees of success, but I don't identify them the way society does. Society views success on two levels, and I see those levels as macro and micro. The macro level of success is what the individual has accomplished on a large scale that can be measured by the accumulation of wealth, which can influence the Gross National Product, national/international notoriety, and sometimes the person's legacy.

On the micro level, success is on a smaller scale and the individual isn't widely known and perhaps hasn't attained much wealth.

I believe that success can't be so narrowly defined, that humans are diverse beings and because of this diversity we cannot be limited to only macro and micro levels. I see success as multi-layered and multi-dimensional, encompassing many levels including spirituality, family, community, etc.

For most people, success takes on different meanings at different stages of their lives. For instance, a teenage boy might view success as getting good grades, being popular, having the trendiest clothes, and dating beautiful girls.

Some years ago I worked with public housing residents who were asthma sufferers and their community had a high number of asthmatic children. We knew that their environment contributed to and even exacerbated their asthma, so we began a campaign to mobilize other residents and raise public awareness of this issue.

The advocacy and education campaign resulted in many positive outcomes, one being the placement of a monitoring station in their community that was used to measure the amount of pollution in the air. This was indeed a success on a community level, which stemmed from a few individuals' frustration with their environment and personal struggle with their health. It also had a positive impact and has made a remarkable difference in the lives of many citizens.

Unfortunately, many people only aspire for the macro level of success because it is believed to be the ideal level. But we should seek only the levels of success we have defined for ourselves.

Wright

How has an attuned sense of intuition led to success in your personal and professional life?

George-Feres

Let me first say that faith set me on the path of success, but intuition has kept me here. My intuition has provided me with a clear sense of direction that most often will keep me from unproductive things, and believe me, there are many times when I could have done unproductive things in my life! So it keeps me from choosing that kind of path, and keeps me closer to where I need to be. It not only provides me with accurate information every time, but it's available to me when I need it the most.

Being highly attuned has helped me to be prepared for changes on the horizon, and assists me to better predict problems and prepare for them. It helps me to think "outside of the box." I say that because I find myself solving problems in different ways and using a different level of consciousness to solve them. And it also helps me to attain a fresh perspective on any situation.

The most important change in myself that I've realized since I've been using my intuition is that I pay far closer attention to my environment. Most importantly, it has enabled me to build positive relationships—a fundamental element of success.

But you know, this attuned sense hasn't always been there. I had to develop it over time, and happily I was able to do so; I am still cultivating this sixth sense. Furthermore, I'm constantly working hard to stay attuned. It gets easier now to do so than before. Nevertheless there are strong forces that often pull me off my intuitive center just as fear, anxiety, logic, values, and those kinds of culprits often try to silence the messages from my intuition.

My understanding of my personal and professional success is constantly changing because as I evolve, my paradigm shifts and causes me to change my definition of success. However, my approach to success remains the same. And that approach is to harness the power of my intuition (I like to call it "my sixth sense") to receive the clarity, the knowledge, and guidance so that I can deal with whatever situation comes my way.

Wright

Using your creative approach, what advice would you give to someone who wants to be a leader in his or her industry?

George-Feres

To be a leader you must first understand the responsibility of leadership. As a leader in your industry you must respond promptly to challenges and opportunities, master change, and be receptive to new ideas. Secondly, you must use your power wisely to influence others, promote a common purpose, show appreciation for others' achievements, develop other leaders, and build and share knowledge. In addition, there are ten tools to help you gain a leading edge in your industry. These tools have worked well for me and for others that I have shared them with.

The first tool is to consult your intuition for guidance. Consulting your intuition allows you to figure out your next best move.

Second, examine the industry's economic climate, general business forecast, trends, analyze the information, and take risks; but more importantly, plan to win.

The third is make decisions based upon your long-term leadership vision, not merely on day-to-day tasks. Seek out new information that enhances your skill sets and knowledge. Develop creative ways to maximize and make effective use of your resources. Build "Strategic Partnerships." Building Strategic Partnerships means you are engaging in partnerships that help you to increase profits, visibility, or access new resources.

The remaining tools are to identify potential issues and neutralize them before they materialize, focus on solutions, even if they counter conventional methods, build a strong team, and lastly, design a growth strategy integrating all the key elements of success.

Wright

So how does your approach to achieving success in leadership and business differ from other approaches?

George-Feres

My approach is simply one of many effective approaches, but what makes it uniquely different is its uncanny method. Harnessing intuition is a holistic approach for building a successful life. Unlike any other approaches, the Harness

Intuition approach is very simple. It integrates all of the thinking styles such as logic, rational reasoning, etc., and synthesizes them into compelling messages.

Your intuition is very accurate and precise; if used appropriately it is mistake free. For those who are unfamiliar with the way intuition works, it may seem strange to understand and to some degree, merely unnatural. Thankfully, this approach teaches people the guidelines for being attuned and provide the tools for harnessing their intuition. This is specifically for men whose preferred style of thinking is logical and linear.

As mentioned earlier, most of us are thought to use logic, inductive, and deductive reasoning, fact-finding, or other traditional modes of thinking to decipher life. And these modes usually come in the medium of hard data; however, intuition focuses purely on the other side of the mind that is rarely used. It also helps to develop emotional intelligence, which is the capacity to reason with emotions and to use emotions to enhance thinking. The discovery of this new type of intelligence is said to be "equally as important as our cognitive intelligence."

Despite its benefits and value, for some individuals (especially those who are business leaders), this approach may lack value because it is rather implicit—not very tangible. They may view it as an additional challenge because they can't use their intuition in the same way they can use physical documents consisting of data, trends, or projections. Therefore, making strategic business decisions based on intuition goes against the conventional way decisions are made in business. Without a tangible source, a business leader may find it difficult to convince others to proceed or lead them in a specific direction if he or she hasn't the data to support his or her recommendation. Therefore, when it comes to business, the culture really mandates that we only rely on quantifiable data or research to make strategic business decisions, so the use of intuition in business is often disregarded. However, we should begin to explore this approach because of its usefulness, reliability, timeliness, and accuracy.

Wright

What do you think is the intuition blueprint for success?

George-Feres

The intuition blueprint for success is a simple formula. It isn't a long laundry list of to-dos. But what it requires is a commitment to the process, a shift in thinking, and self-trust. The blueprint was derived from years of research and my life experiences. The blueprint is: Intuition + Logic + Knowledge + Resources = Success. There are four simple steps to this blueprint:

- Harness your intuition to stimulate ideas, discover new approaches, improve decisiveness, and excel at empowering others.
- Use a combination of intuition and logic. Doing so will help you to interpret information clearly and enable you to take action without undue haste or delay.
- Build knowledge, strengthen weaknesses, consider innovative possibilities, and display a high degree of integrity. And Lastly,
- Create a success-based strategy that advances your growth, capitalize on opportunities, and turn past failures into future success.

On the surface, it may appear that the steps in the blueprint are a cookie-cutter approach to success. But if you examine it more in depth what you will find is an innovative guide to building a successful life. The first step in the blueprint directs you to your intuition. Use it to unveil underlying issues that inhibit success, develop a clearer understanding of what is standing in your way, and address it before it sabotages your progress. So if you appropriately utilize your intuition, the outcome will be an innovative and customized blueprint that guides your day-to-day actions and decisions.

In closing, I encourage you to take stock in the hunches, gut feelings, or physical sensations you receive on a daily basis. By doing so, you will place more emphasis on the intuitive messages. I urge you to take an inventory of all the messages you have received from your intuition in the past, but have ignored. Sit in a quiet place and identify how many of those messages have turned out to be accurate. Try testing the accuracy of the messages by validating them. An easy way to do this is to find any tangible evidence—past or present—that proves their accuracy. This activity will not only demonstrate the validity of your intuition, but, hopefully, will convince you to begin trusting your intuition. My desire is for you to effectively utilize your intuition in everyday business practice, as well as in your personal life.

You can solve any difficulties, attract meaningful relationships, create positive change, and find success by harnessing the power of your intuition. As you have read through this chapter, I hope you have now begun your self-transformation. Don't let this word scare you, it doesn't mean you must change your ideology, what it means is that you've now opened yourself up to a new level of understanding of your inner wisdom and have furthered your learning of its value. However, the real transformation begins when you are utilizing your intuition on a daily basis and establishing a higher state of consciousness. I'd like to share a power thought that may be helpful to you during this transformation process. It comes from one of my favorite authors Louise Hay, author of *You Can Heal Your Life*:

"As I go about my daily affairs, I listen to my own guidance. My intuition is always on my side. I trust it to be there at all times. I am safe."

As you go about your life attending to matters of the heart, addressing issues, challenges, and contemplating your next strategic move, let your intuition be your guide. Why limit yourself to conventional information, why not utilize the clarity, accuracy and timeliness of your most powerful tool, your intuition. Using your intuition will elevate you to a higher state of consciousness and unlock your true inner potential that would lead you to success.

About Deborah George-Feres...

DEBORAH GEORGE-FERES is a Certified Coach and founder of InDiGo Coaching Systems (ICS), a firm specializing in personal and organizational development. She is known for her intuitive abilities and personal development strategies that she utilizes in her coaching practice to help her clients achieve personal success. Prior to founding ICS, Deborah worked with city mayors across the nation to develop strategies for growth and success in their jurisdictions. She co-founded the Boston Urban Asthma Coalition and recently created the InDiGo Entrepreneur Foundation that equips fledging entrepreneurs with the knowledge, tools, and resources to grow their businesses and execute their plans. Deborah possesses a Masters of Science degree in Community Economic Development from Southern New Hampshire University and a Bachelor of Arts in Business Administration from Eastern Nazarene College.

Deborah George-Feres
InDiGo Coaching Systems
Crofton, MD 21114
443.567.1904
info@indigocoachingsystems.com
www.indigocoachingsystems.com

Chapter **Ten**

An interview with...

Ruby Newell-Legner

David Wright (Wright)

Today we're talking with Ruby Newell-Legner. She founded RubySpeaks, Inc. in 1994 with a singular mission: to provide the hands-on training employees need to create a work environment where everyone can excel on the job. As a leading expert in customer satisfaction, Ruby was selected to train the guest relations staff for Super Bowl XLI and the 2010 Olympic venues in Vancouver, British Columbia, Canada.

Ruby's background includes more than two decades as a coach, teacher, professional speaker, and facility manager. Today she helps organizations create cultures that deliver exceptional customer service and helps employees get excited about their jobs. As a trainer and performance consultant, she works with organizations to build better relationships between front-line employees and customers, between co-workers and their peers, and between managers and the employees they supervise.

Ruby lives in Littleton, Colorado, and travels worldwide. In the last thirteen years she has presented more than 1,700 training programs in nine countries.

Ruby, welcome to *Blueprint for Success!*

Ruby Newell-Legner (Newell-Legner)

Thank you, David.

Wright

Ruby, how do you define success?

Newell-Legner

Oh without a doubt it's loving what you do and being so passionate about it that you can't wait to get up every day so you can get started!

Wright

Is that true for you?

Newell-Legner

Absolutely! I love my job; I'm the luckiest woman in the world. My goal really is to help others avoid the frustration and the mistakes I experienced as I was promoted up the chain of command. So I offer training programs that help employees get the tools they need to succeed. Sometimes it's basic customer service skills and sometimes it's management and leadership training.

Wright

That is quite a worthy mission. Where did it come from?

Newell-Legner

As a front-line employee I was always good at my job—so much so that they put me in charge and that is where my struggles began. You see, I was never taught what a good manager should do. As a brand new supervisor, I just learned by trial and error. I am sure there are some employees who had me early on as a boss and, as a result, are in therapy today. I was awful to work for. Luckily I improved along the way.

Today I help supervisors become successful before they get promoted. I help prepare them for more responsibility before they are put in charge. If they can understand a few basic strategies, they start off on the right foot.

Wright

What would some of those strategies be?

Newell-Legner

My most important strategy is clarifying your expectations for your staff. I also encourage them to be a positive role model, offer developmental not punitive support, and communicate, communicate, communicate!

Wright

Tell me more about clarifying expectations. That seems like a no-brainer to me.

Newell-Legner

I specialize in guest relations and customer service. Quite often I go into organizations and provide "secret shopping" before presenting their training sessions. During my observations, I see employees missing the simplest things that can help them deliver great service. When I ask them why they didn't do those things, I frequently get the answer, "No one ever told me I was supposed to do that."

There are basic rules in customer service, and once front-line employees learn those rules they can really shine. They also like their jobs better because they aren't frustrated every day by trying to meet the demands of high-maintenance patrons. We all like to look smart; when employees know how to respond to requests or deal with upset customers, they feel good about what they do and their jobs become easier.

There are just too many employees out there who hate their jobs, and a lot of it has to do with their lack of training.

Wright

What else causes them to hate their jobs?

Newell-Legner

Oh, there's a long list on that one. I sometimes see double standards in how leaders act and what they expect of their employees. Sometimes they don't even know they're being bad examples for their employees. In my leadership programs I explain, "Your employees will treat your customers like you treat your staff." That revelation always gets their attention. Sometimes they reflect back on a recent conversation they had with a staff member and I watch them sink down into their chair when they realize they really aren't "practicing what they preach."

Wright

What other words of wisdom would you have to help supervisors be successful?

Newell-Legner

Sometimes supervisors believe that employees are choosing to do things incorrectly just to irritate their bosses. But in reality, they aren't doing things right because they don't know how. I encourage supervisors to take a look at employees and decide what skill hasn't been developed that is causing the employees to do something wrong. Then it's up to the supervisor to find a teachable moment to help the employees learn in a way that gets them excited about learning a new skill. The supervisor has to create an atmosphere where they want to learn new things without shoving it down their throats. There are lots of nuances that go along with the scenario for the transfer of learning to take place.

Wright

What would some of those nuances be?

Newell-Legner

Trust has to be established between the supervisor and the employee, and that's done early on in the relationship. If the employee can't trust his or her boss, then there is no relationship. A key ingredient in the learning environment is that positive relationship with the supervisor.

One of my favorite quotes is by Chris Widener. He says, "Your success as a leader will be determined by your ability to influence." The first time I heard that I thought there was a word missing—influence what? The more I thought about it, the more I agreed with Chris. Your success as a supervisor will be determined by your ability to influence your staff to perform. Giving them the tools to perform is part of your responsibility as a supervisor. Sometimes I see employees who are just frustrated and doing all the wrong things, but they've not had the opportunity to learn from their boss—they haven't developed that mentor relationship. When that mentor relationship is there, then it's a teamwork approach.

Wright

What other suggestions would you have for supervisors who want to become successful?

Newell-Legner

One of the biggest things is to invest in self-development and invest in employee development as well. If supervisors and managers share their vision clearly, invite their staff to be part of that vision, offer the tools to help them build that vision, and reward positive performance, there is a good chance that vision will come to fruition. But rarely does that happen. I think this is partly because some leaders don't have a clear vision of what they are striving for, they can't articulate it, or they choose not to—and certainly if they don't know what it is then they can't share it with their staff. A lot of times if you go in and ask the staff, "What do you think your boss expects of you?" they just don't know how to reply. Getting to know yourself as a leader can be the key step in helping you and your staff go up the ladder of success.

Wright

What advice would you have for leaders who want to be successful?

Newell-Legner

Their success will be based on how they treat others around them. That goes for coworkers, people they supervise, clients they work with, or customers they serve. I encourage leaders to work on themselves first—to develop positive rapport skills. Become a better listener and learn to relate to everyone around you, and it will be a great step in furthering your career. I believe that positive communication is essential for leaders to succeed. And communication isn't always talking; a lot of the time it's listening and really showing sincere interest.

Wright

What role models do you have for great communicators?

Newell-Legner

The first one that comes to mind is Stephen Covey, and he is without a doubt my favorite. I think I wore out two sets of CDs of *Seven Habits of Highly Effective People*. I listened to that program over and over and he truly shows his compassion and his caring—it comes through with every sentence. He wants to help you become better, and he's a joy to learn from! His teachings are based on his life experiences and he isn't ashamed to share errors that he made along the way so that we can learn from them.

Wright

Is that something you do in your programs?

Newell-Legner

By all means, I am on a mission to help others avoid the mistakes I made so I am not bashful about sharing my mistakes, and I've got *lots* of material there—especially if it can provide the groundwork for a lesson they need to learn. There is nothing more exciting for me than watching audience members listen to my journey and then go on their own mental journeys to apply the lesson. I can almost see those light bulbs above their heads, and when they start glowing that creates the excitement factor for me.

Wright

Since public speaking is the number one challenge that everyone has, I'm always interested in this next question—what got you into speaking?

Newell-Legner

You're right; there is a lot of fear in getting up in front of an audience. It wasn't easy for me when I first started speaking, but I had a good incentive. For twenty years I lived my dream of being a swim coach. After graduating from college with a minor in coaching, I looked for jobs that would support my coaching habit and allow me to make enough to pay the rent. First I became a teacher and then a recreation facility manager. I treasured the opportunity to help children and young adults enjoy the sport of swimming. It offered valuable lessons in dedication, perseverance, and goal setting—the success factors.

About five years before I ended my career I developed HP (hypersensitivity pneumonitis), a chronic condition that caused frequent sinus infections, a terrible cough, and major headaches. It was a serious problem for me; people would hear me cough and think I was going to die any minute. I visited many doctors to finally get diagnosed and then one day I was told that if I wanted to get healthy I had to get out of the pool environment. Well, it's difficult to coach swimming when you're not in the pool! So I decided to figure out another way to motivate people.

Because I absolutely loved coaching, I thought if I can't coach on the pool deck maybe I can coach from another venue. So I started exploring public speaking and found out that I really liked it. I'm an adrenaline junkie anyway, and I love the "rush" I get from getting up in front of a group.

It was very challenging when I first started; at my first national convention I did a ninety-minute program in forty-five minutes! I don't think I took a breath the whole entire time. Over the years it's gotten much easier for me, but that first big step was coming home one day and telling my husband, "I want to quit my job and be a professional speaker," and luckily I'm married to the man of my dreams and he was very, very supportive. We sat down and started a tradition fourteen years ago that we still do to this day—we knew we were going to go through a major change as I embarked on a new career and we needed to set out on the right course. On New Year's Day we now have a tradition in which we sit down and set goals together. We write down what we want to do, and of course the first time we did it he thought, "Oh boy, here we go," and he said, "You've been to a seminar, haven't you?" And I said, "Yes, and we're going to do this because I know I want to quit my job and we need to set some goals to make that happen." The second year he brought goals to the meeting, and since then it's been a tradition year after year. We post the goals where we can both refer to them frequently, and we work toward achieving them together. It has really helped us stay happily married all these years and we just celebrated our twentieth wedding anniversary.

Swimming was so important to me that it took a huge jump in my frame of mind to think about doing something else for a living. To put it in perspective for you, I was so into swimming that our wedding was on a Sunday between Junior National Swimming Championships and Senior National Swimming Championships—my husband thought he would lift up my veil and find me holding the clipboard and the stopwatch! Swimming was pretty much my life, so I needed to find something to replace that passion. I also needed the people around me to support my endeavors as well.

Wright

That doesn't sound like that was very easy for you. What steps did you take to make the transition?

Newell-Legner

First, I had to get off the "WAHmbulance" (driven by those people who moan and complain about everything). I was driving the WAHmbulance about having to quit coaching swimming because it truly was my life. And so I quit feeling sorry for myself and redirected my energies; I decided that if any change was going to come about, I had to make that change. Then things started looking a lot better, and that was fourteen years ago. Not long after that, I decided to join the National Speakers Association and start taking classes on communication and public speaking so I could get comfortable in front of the audience. It literally took me two years to learn how to breathe on stage! Today it's much easier for me and I feel so blessed. Who knew I could find a replacement career that I would love even more than coaching swimming?

The beauty of my job is that I get to travel around the world and help organizations improve their workplace. Whether I am working with Jumeirah

Group (a leader in hospitality in Dubai, United Arab Emirates), providing training for GE in India and Singapore, or working with local park and recreation agencies, they all have one thing in common: they strive to create a great environment for their workers so that their employees will create positive experiences for their customers. Whether I am working with the management team for a stadium or front-line staff members at an amusement park, the theme is the same: find out what skills need to be developed and work toward helping the individuals learn those skills.

Wright

What was the main thing that helped you be successful in this career as a speaker and consultant?

Newell-Legner

Without a doubt it is my ability to look at things from another perspective. It is the best gift my mother gave me. She had a knack for always seeing the bright side of things. No matter what happened, mom could turn it around and make it a *good* thing. Later on in my years I decided to call it "the flip-flop" because anytime she was faced with what could easily be a negative situation, she would turn it into a positive!

Sometimes, you just have to step back and force yourself to look at life another way, and if you try hard enough you can see the positive light of almost any situation. That one skill has helped me more than anything. I live by that upbeat perspective and it helps me get through every day and any challenge that I may be confronted with.

Wright

How do you use "the flip flop" with your clients?

Newell-Legner

Sometimes they are too close to a situation, and as an outsider I can offer another way to look at things. I ask lots of questions and sometimes those questions help clients discover their own "ah-has." Those are the moments I like best, when it's a group project that's a journey working side-by-side with somebody to help him or her be successful.

You have to *partner* with clients to help them become successful. Whether I am working with meeting planners for special engagements for association meetings, or with leaders trying to take their organizations to the next level, my goal is to stand beside them and make them look good. We are a team, and the best end result is when everyone wins. It's back to the Stephen Covey philosophy of having a win-win philosophy.

Wright

In closing our conversation today, what final thoughts would you like to share with our readers about success?

Newell-Legner

The biggest words of wisdom I can offer are these: Find a job that you love and then you will never have to work a day in your life—you'll enjoy every single day and you'll feel passionate about your life's work. For me that is helping people. Life is too short to be stuck in a job that you don't like, and I encourage people who are in a job that they don't like to *get out of that spot!* Someone else wants it and there is a great new opportunity out there just waiting for you. Sometimes people stay in a job way too long just because they're afraid of taking that risk. So do what I did. I didn't quit my day job—I kept my day job for two and a half years once I decided I wanted to become a speaker, and that built up my confidence and some clientele so that when I did quit my job it wasn't so devastating to me, especially financially.

If you are in a less than perfect job, figure out how it can be the catalyst to take you to a more desirable position. If you like your job but are frustrated by how challenging it is, go get some help, get some training. Self-improvement is the best investment you can make in your future.

About Ruby Newell-Legner

RUBY NEWELL-LEGNER, Certified Speaking Professional, is an internationally recognized training expert in the leisure, sports, and entertainment industry. She helps organizations build strong teams between front-line staff and management and helps them establish exceptional customer service as a way of life. Ruby's high-impact trainings are based on twenty-five years as a front-line service provider and facility manager. With "in the trenches" practical know-how, she has an uncommon level of experience that gives immediate credibility with front-line staff as well as the top leaders of the organization.

Ruby has worked together with her clients to build workplace learning programs for some of the largest, most recognized organizations in the country. Her track record in satisfying clients is evidenced by the number of clients who have hired Ruby again and again to provide training for their group. With expertise in the areas of leadership, management, and internal and external customer service, Ruby provides new perspectives and fresh ideas that enhance ongoing initiatives to create both immediate and lasting results.

Ruby's knowledge of industry best practices and customer service standards is one reason why many of the top leisure entertainment providers in the world have asked Ruby to provide staff training. She has helped staff in venues such as Six Flags Amusement Parks and Wild Wadi Water Park in Dubai reflect her vision for customer service. She has also provided staff training for major events including Super Bowl XLI, the Grey Cup, and the 2010 Olympics.

Ruby Newell-Legner, CSP
RubySpeaks, Inc.
9148 W. Vandeventor Drive
Littleton, CO 80128
303.933.9291
Ruby@RubySpeaks.com
www.RubySpeaks.com
www.GuestRelationsTraining.com

Chapter Eleven

An interview with...

David Coleman

David Wright (Wright)

Today we're talking with David Coleman who is internationally known as "The Dating Doctor" and "America's Real-Life Hitch." He has been honored eleven times as *America's National Campus Speaker of the Year*. David is a highly sought-after speaker, entertainer, emcee, author, leadership trainer, retreat facilitator, and radio and television personality. He has keynoted for some of America's top corporations, and appeared at thousands of colleges and civic groups speaking live to over two million people. David lives by the motto, "Where is it said that learning can't be fun and entertainment can't be life-changing?" In any and every capacity, David Coleman changes lives!

David, welcome to *Blueprint for Success!*

David Coleman (Coleman)

Thank you very much for inviting me to be a part of this wonderful project. I am honored and humbled to be included.

Wright

You are referred to as "The Dating Doctor" and "America's Real-Life Hitch," please elaborate as to why and how this came about.

Coleman

As a speaker and entertainer I have been helping people's social lives, work lives, romantic lives, and personal lives since 1985. The monikers the "Dating Doctor" and "America's Real-life Hitch" were derived from a program I created several years back called "Creative Dating." I presented it at high schools, college campuses, and civic groups, etc. It focused on how to break the ice and ask someone out on a date and provided simple dating ideas that would be affordable yet effective. I also dispensed advice about how to begin the process of courting someone—a lost art in this country. Add the fact that I live in Loveland, Ohio, and the title "The Dating Doctor" was born. I applied for and received legal protection for the name and have been using it ever since.

The first big break in my career occurred while I was attending a rather large conference in Washington, D.C., in February 1985. A snowstorm caused travel havoc that day and the keynote speaker wasn't able to make it to the convention. The conference chair walked out on stage and said, "We have a problem—tonight's speaker couldn't make it due to inclement weather and is stuck in New York. Unless somebody has something to discuss, I think we are going to have to cancel this evening's program." For thirty seconds or so the audience was mumbling and then, in front of three thousand people, I stood up and said, "I recently created a program on dating, relationships, romance, sex, marriage, and divorce, and if you give me ten minutes to prepare I'd be happy to share it with the audience."

The room began to buzz. This was before Dr. Phil or Dr. Laura, or Dr. Judy became famous for speaking on these topics so the idea was a novel one. They accepted my offer and gave me an hour to speak to the entire delegation. Immediately following my talk I booked several dozen appearances before I even left the room! You have to be rare to be recognized and on that night, I took my shot and was.

Another break occurred that night and proved that serendipity can be a wonderful thing. When I'm on stage speaking, people have fun; they're learning but there's also a great deal of laughter involved. Three women (all good friends) were walking through the hotel and heard laughter emanating from somewhere inside the hotel. Curious, they followed the laughter and ended up standing in the back of the ballroom where I was speaking. They loved my program and message. It turned out that one was a writer for the *Chronicle of Higher Education,* one freelanced for the *Washington Post,* and the other wrote for *Glamour* magazine. They sent for a photographer, they each took turns interviewing me, and each one of those publications ran a highly complimentary story on me. The rest, as they say, is history.

The role that actor Will Smith played in the movie *Hitch* is so similar to my own life experiences and what I do for a living that Sony Motion Pictures hired me to conduct a worldwide promotional campaign for the movie. It is mysteriously uncanny how closely the movie parallels my life. People ask me all the time how much of the movie is true and how much of it is Hollywood. Well, I never kicked a woman off a jet ski into the middle of the Hudson River. I never ferried a woman to Ellis Island to point out that her great-great-grandfather was a mass murderer. But there was a part where the Hitch character's face swells after he experienced an allergic reaction while eating seafood and that *did* happen to me, however, my face looked even worse than his did!

I do help people find love, so the "America's Real-Life Hitch" moniker was also attached to me because I work with individual clients like he did in the hit movie. Most people are simply standing in their own way and I try to open a door so that they can walk on through and achieve the satisfaction they desire. I've also been called the "Advisor to the Romantically Challenged." No matter the tag line, the bottom line is that my goal is to help people replace confusion with clarity, and loneliness with love.

Wright

Regardless of the dynamics, who controls a relationship between any two people?

Coleman

Whenever I speak to a group or work with a client, this is the one area that resonates the most with people. The person who loves, cares, or tries the *least*—the one who is *least* invested—has the most control because the one who is more invested has to work twice as hard to keep the other person interested and to keep the relationship going. I call this situation "The Puppy Theory of Relationships."

If you have a young puppy, it will mess up on the floor upon occasion until it is fully housebroken. When an accident occurs, you don't encourage the animal by saying, "Good puppy! Good puppy! Please do that again!" We all know better than to reinforce a negative behavior. Rather, you take the pet by the collar, firmly push its nose toward the spot or pile, and say, "No. Don't do that again!" I don't suggest that people go home and defecate or urinate on their floor and attempt to take someone's nose and rub it in it, but every day that we allow others to treat us with disrespect, yet they still get *everything* they want, desire, or expect from us, they receive the message that the behavior is acceptable—that is unacceptable. It "trains" them and encourages them to repeat the use of negative words and actions. So once again, it's the person who's least invested that has the control in a relationship.

Wright

Are there common characteristics found in successful healthy relationships, regardless of where those relationships occur?

Coleman

Let me begin by sharing the difference between a "healthy" and an "unhealthy" relationship. In a healthy relationship, the stronger person (meaning the person who is stronger of body, mind, and spirit at that particular time) takes *care* of the weaker person until the weaker person is strong enough on his or her own to be self-sufficient. As human beings, we waver throughout our lives and over time individuals may be stronger or weaker at one time or another.

In an unhealthy relationship the stronger person takes *advantage* of the weaker person to keep him or her down, dependent, and under control. In the mind of the abuser, the longer he or she can keep the weaker person dependent, the more important and invaluable he or she becomes to that person. Consider it a skewed version of relationship security.

There are five characteristics associated with healthy relationships—be it a romantic relationship, interactions between colleagues, or service between a company and its clients. Each of these characteristics transcends every single human interaction. The letters form the acronym, TRIPC, whereby each individual letter stands for one of the characteristics found in a healthy relationship.

The T stands for Trust, which is the confidence to believe that a person's words and actions will be what he or she says they will be.

The R stands for Respect, which is mutual, equal, and earned.

The I stands for Intimacy, which is often mistaken for some type of physical interaction. It can actually encompass eye contact, romantic gestures, sense of humor, closeness of spirit, or appreciation of time spent together. You and I are having an intimate conversation right now, so intimacy is between two people— one-on-one—or a group sharing time or an experience that is unique to them.

The P stands for Passion. The passion in romantic relationships can be physical or heartfelt. The passion shared by employees may be for their work, their careers, their clients, or being part of a team where no one cares who gets the credit.

And the C stands for Commitment—an unwavering, unconditional bond that stands the test of time.

In a healthy relationship you're looking for trust, respect, intimacy, passion, and commitment.

Wright

Your corporate program is titled "Happy People Produce, Unhappy People Make an Excuse!" What is the underlying premise of this program?

Coleman

If people are unhappy or dissatisfied with the quality of their personal, social, or romantic lives, it will absolutely affect the nature of how well they perform their jobs. Whether they are married or single, separated or divorced, straight or gay, if they are frustrated or dissatisfied at home, they may become pre-occupied, distant, or distracted at work. They might become moody, skeptical of new ideas or change, or they might become jealous of a colleague's success. They could become flirtatious, experience increased absenteeism, or develop into a workaholic. In their mind, the busier they keep themselves, the less time they have time to experience the loneliness and desperation they feel. People may immerse themselves in their jobs as they lack someone with whom to share and process life's experiences.

A company's bottom line can and will be negatively affected as a result of burn-out, loss of productivity, diminished creativity, lack of teamwork, or a void of energy and enthusiasm. It also affects customer service, which is about maintaining a positive attitude, being prompt, and going the extra mile. It has been proven time and again that countless dollars are lost each year in corporate America due to employees' dissatisfaction within their own personal lives and how it affects their ability to remain active, positive, and reliable at work.

It doesn't have to be that way. If you ask the leaders of most businesses they will say that they perceive the personal, social, and romantic lives of their employees to be off-limits and taboo. But that's the beauty of my program and message. I help each individual employee in all of the areas they are lacking in a way that allows them to maintain complete confidentiality, learn at their own pace, and share as much or as little as they desire. It will have a positive impact on each person without ever having to disclose information he or she would consider personal. It is intended to build a framework to support the strongest possible relationships and foster continued growth in all aspects of a person's life.

I also address the elimination of self-fulfilling prophecies. Far too many people live their lives encompassed in a cloud of negativity. They wake up and convince themselves that they are not good enough, talented enough, attractive enough, or successful enough. They criticize themselves from the moment they arise and then wonder why the relationships in their lives aren't more successful!

I cover the stages of relationships, the stages of married life, and the three types of love found in healthy and loving relationships. We discuss the five characteristics found in healthy relationships, which I previously mentioned—the stages of dating and relating after divorce—and methods to maintain a true balance of body, mind, and spirit so that you're prepared for any relationship that may present itself. It is fun, fast-paced, and life changing.

Wright

You've said it should not take a long time to ascertain whether or not a relationship is worth pursuing. Please explain the "Five Minute Find" and the "ABC's of Initial Interest."

Coleman

Ever since the movie *Hitch* was released the most common question I hear from my clients or an audience is, "How can we be sure, in the shortest time possible, whether or not someone is worth pursuing? How can we tell if a person is worth marrying or becoming physically intimate with?" So I developed a model called "The Five Minute Find." It doesn't take five days, five weeks, five months, or five years to ascertain whether or not someone is worth pursuing—it takes five minutes!

There's an A, B, C, and D, and that's why it is called the ABC's of Initial Interest.

The first characteristic you look for (the A) is Attraction. There should be some type of immediate interest in the other person physically. Hopefully, you won't meet them and feel repulsed or completely disinterested.

The B stands for Believability. When he or she is speaking to you, what is being said and how is it being communicated? Do the words ring sincere, true, and genuine to you, or do you sense that the person may be lying to you, fabricating a story, or trying to top you or impress you? You want to believe what you are hearing and experience an ease of communication with someone.

The C stands for Chemistry. People ask me repeatedly if Chemistry is the same as Attraction. The answer is no. You might find someone to be exceptionally stunning or handsome, but the more you talk with the person and get to know him or her, you feel no interest beyond the physical. Chemistry is every other aspect of attraction other than physical. Did you feel comfortable around the person? Was the communication effortless? Did you discover mutual interests? Did he or she make you laugh? Think? Challenge you? Did time fly by? Those are all elements of Chemistry!

The D stands for Desire. Again, it's not the desire to marry, it's not the desire to immediately engage physically, it is simply the desire to get to know the person better and see him or her again.

The Five Minute Find and the ABC's of Initial Interest are Attraction, Believability, Chemistry, and Desire. If you sense these in the first five or ten minutes, should you pursue establishing a relationship? I believe so—at least for a first or second date and then progress from there.

Wright

If you feel that you've become someone's "Plan B" in life, in love, or at work, what does that mean? And can it be challenged or changed?

Coleman

"Plan B" means you have been put on layaway. You have allowed another person to take you "off the market" from anyone who might be interested in pursuing a relationship with you, hiring you, or promoting you. As an employee it may manifest in your being told, "We've got big plans for you!" in order to keep you from taking another job or to keep you pacified while the company decides the best course of action to take regarding your future. In a romantic relationship, it is much the same. Someone has led you to believe that he or she is interested in you, but for some reason the person cannot or will not act upon the interest, however, the person may say something like, "If you will just be patient, it will happen eventually."

It's the same as walking into a store and having an item catch your attention. You are interested but are hesitant to make the purchase at that particular time. So, you ask the store personnel to put it on layaway for you. Rarely do we return to the store and purchase the item in question. We may find an item in another store that we like better. We might forget that we put it on layaway in the first place. We ponder at the ramifications of the purchase and decide against it. The list of why we never follow through on purchases is endless.

There's a saying, "If you have a bird in a cage and you let it go, if it comes back to you, it was meant to be yours forever." Never forget that if you let the bird out it can meet a new bird, get blown off course, or forget its way home. Many things could change. The same holds true if you allow people to make you their Plan B and put you on layaway—the odds are they will *never* come back and make you a top priority because they don't have to as you aren't going anywhere.

The reason that people repeat poor decisions in their life is because they seek out what is familiar to them, and what they practice they become good at. The longer they practice making you their "Plan B," and the longer you allow it to happen, the easier it becomes for everyone involved to maintain the status quo.

Wright

Are there stages people progress through and strategies that they should employ to successfully navigate a divorce and begin socializing again?

Coleman

There sure are, and the most rapidly rising segment of my work involves divorced individuals. I have found that there are five very distinct stages people progress through post-divorce as they are looking to get back into the dating scene. Coincidentally, they all begin with the letter F.

The first stage is called the Fear phase. Divorced people seem to experience a time of self-doubt where they believe the only person who will ever want them or be attracted to them is their ex. They believe that they found their soul mate once and it didn't work out, so why should they expect it to work out again? For many divorced individuals, their greatest fear is that they will live alone for the rest of their lives and that no one will want them.

The second stage is referred to as the Freedom phase. It's usually more fun and interesting for most people, as during this phase people go out on dates and undertake activities they wanted to do when they were married or spoken for but couldn't because it would not have been appropriate. So, people go a bit crazy. They may date a multitude of people in a short period of time or may have always wanted to date someone with certain physical characteristics and thus they do. Perhaps they fantasized about dating someone in a certain profession or they dreamed of traveling extensively and visiting exotic places with a certain person and thus they do just that.

Once the Freedom phase has passed, and it will pass, people will begin to focus on finding one or two people with whom they feel a true connection. Thus the next stage is called the Finding Phase. People attempt to go from dating many to dating one or two people who they perceive have the potential to bring them long-term happiness and stability. During this phase, people attempt to reduce their choices down to just one person and begin the Forming Phase whereby they bond with just one person and become much closer over time. During the forming phase people attempt to increase their level of communication and their level of comfort as they challenge and support one another. If they believe the other person is the one they are truly looking for, they will begin to finalize the relationship, which is the ending phase.

So the stages of dating after divorce are: the Fear phase, the Freedom phase, the Finding phase, the Forming phase, and the Finalizing phase.

Wright

Are there standard guidelines or minimum standards people should follow if they socialize or enter into relationships online?

Coleman

Online dating is an increasingly popular method of how people in this country (and the world) are choosing to meet one another. On-line dating encompasses everything from joining a dating service to becoming a member of MySpace or Facebook, sending e-mail, text messaging, or sharing moments via cellular phones with video or photo capability. There are several concrete strategies people should employ when dating on-line or relying upon electronics to drive their relationship.

First, they have to display honest pictures of themselves wherever they are posted. For over a year I dated on-line, so I can speak from experience on this topic. I once met a woman for a lunch date who ended up being two hundred and fifty pounds larger than the pictures she had posted online. When I inquired as to why she misled me and others on her profile, she replied, "I didn't think you'd meet me if I posted accurate pictures of myself." I explained to her that she had just begun a relationship based upon deceit and deception, and that was not going to lead to a healthy and productive connection between her and anyone. Everyone has types that they are drawn to and we just might be someone's type as long as we honestly display who we are.

So people have to display pictures that truthfully portray the way they look and should also answer their profile questions honestly so that others can learn about their preferences and style. They should keep their answers succinct, incorporate some humor, and exhibit the different aspects of their personality and what makes them unique.

The single best advice I can share, if you are going to date online, is to avoid being politically correct when completing your own profile. This country has become so concerned with political correctness that at times it paralyzes people and they fail to do or say what their heart tells them is right.

No matter what online agency you choose, you will be required to answer the questions, "Who am I looking for? What are the characteristics I am looking for in someone I wish to date?" Some people will give in and say they just "don't care"—that "if the person has a pulse, teeth, and a job, I'm in"—but you cannot settle! The potential matches generated for you will be based upon the information you furnished the company. If you seek to date someone with long, dark hair, indicate those characteristics on your profile. If you desire to connect with someone from a certain religion or background, make that clear. If you're looking for a height and weight range, or if there are certain hobbies you're interested in embarking upon, explain that. If you want someone to have a job and make a certain income or you refuse to date a smoker or drinker, indicate as much. If you want to date someone who has children because you do and you want that person to understand the ramifications of dating someone with children, indicate that as your preference. In other words, you have to be extremely precise when indicating the type of person you are seeking to spend time with so that the profiles sent to you are matches based upon compatibility, not simply pictures filling up your computer screen to make you feel wanted.

Wright

You frequently talk about *"The Hmm ... Factor"* and being a "Fat Penguin." Please explain these concepts and why are they are important?

Coleman

The Hmm ... Factor occurs quite often for many people, but the people in question are careful and tactful and rarely articulate their feelings or tip their hand to others. You might be walking to work, going to lunch, working out, or shopping and see a Hmm. You may be attending church or browsing in a bookstore and look up and notice someone you find incredibly attractive. You may or may not be available to meet the person, but in your mind you think, *"Hmm,* that person peaks my interest." Many single, available people have a *Hmm, or several Hmms in mind,* but fail to approach the object of their affection and express interest. Every single day you fail to let a person know that you are interested in him or her, gives that person a chance to meet someone else and never know you.

To solve this problem, I encourage people to become a "Fat Penguin." This has nothing to do with physical appearance—it's about attitude. "Fat Penguins" break the ice! Someone has to do it, and indicate that there is interest—hopefully a mutual interest.

Wright

How can someone make the transformation from being ordinary to becoming remarkable?

Coleman

"Ordinary," is someone or something performing exactly as intended—nothing special, unique, unexpected or exceptional—just the base, bare minimum standards that often go unnoticed and unappreciated. Is there anything wrong with being ordinary? No. The job gets done, it's just that nothing special happens and no one is really noticing. No ones goes the extra mile.

H. J. Heinz—who invented Heinz Ketchup and made condiments a staple of every day life proclaimed, "Something remarkable can be accomplished when someone simply performs a common task uncommonly well."

When working with individual clients whose relationships aren't fairing well, I share some very specific advice. You don't have to be the best looking person or be blessed with six-pack abs or eighteen million dollars in the bank to be a great spouse, partner, boyfriend, or girlfriend. You simply have to err in the direction of romance. For instance, the partner in your life may be facing a terribly hectic day. Your spouse or girlfriend/boyfriend may even have said to you, "I am so busy today that I don't even have time to break for lunch." What would a remarkable person do? Show up at lunchtime, hand him or her a quick meal and ask, "What can I do for you for the next twenty minutes so that you can take a break and eat?"

Again, did it take a great effort to perform this action? No. Was it a common task that was performed uncommonly well? Yes. Was the timing perfect? Yes.

The most common definition of romance is performing an ordinary act of love or kindness at an unexpected time. Want to get your partner's attention? Then do something unexpected—a word or a random act of kindness out of the blue—and you'll see a highly appreciative person.

Holidays are tough, especially for men, and the worst holiday is Valentine's Day. Why? It is difficult to perform an unexpected act when every calendar prominently displays February 14 along with the words "Valentine's Day." And on most calendars, the number 14 is written in red to signify love or romance. I believe the red numbers signify the blood that has been shed by every man who's ever messed up the holiday!

So, to be a hero on the next Valentine's Day, present your gift a day early—on February 13—with a little handwritten note that says, "No one as special as you should have to wait another day." You'll get loving on the 13 *and* the 14, and if you can tell your gift wasn't well received, then simply say, "I was just kidding. I know tomorrow is Valentine's Day!" Then, you have twenty-four hours to shop and save your soul!

Wright

At various points in time, people are returning from military service. What challenges do these individuals face upon returning home and what advice would you give them?

Coleman

Sometimes I'm not the top expert in an area that I'm being asked about, and this is one of those occasions. A dear friend of mine, Alison Lighthall, RN, MS, is the founder of hand2handcontact (www.hand2handcontact.org). She founded H2H in response to the growing psychological impact that overseas operations are having on U.S. service members, and therefore by definition, on our entire country. She has allowed me to share the following information:

When service members return home from deployment, they are often physically, emotionally, psychologically, and spiritual exhausted. They do not have the energy, strength, or interest in repeatedly retelling their stories and answering questions. The majority of these men and women come back feeling they are not the same person as the one who left. They sometimes find it hard to fit back into their lives again.

It's important to know that returning service members don't think of themselves as heroes. We want to look at those people and say, "Oh my gosh, you're my hero." But they consider their fallen comrades or those who remain in action as the true heroes.

Next, be careful not to assume that every military person you might interact with is unified in his or her beliefs politically. Some military personnel are for the war, some are against the war; but it's what they do for a living—being soldiers. And they know that when they took on that role it became their job to do and they did their job to the best of their ability. No matter what their opinions about the war might be, every service member took a solemn oath to uphold the orders of the Commander and Chief and his officers. So if you are going to date someone in the military, you may want to be careful regarding sharing your own political beliefs and opinions. Be cognizant that when you are assailing the President, you are simultaneously criticizing the person who just worked for him and followed his commands.

You may hear a military person say, "I wish I could go back." The last thing you should do is look at that person and say, "Are you crazy?" or "You've got to be kidding! You want to leave and go back to the war?" Until the military person believes that the mission has been accomplished, he or she still has comrades who are there and working very hard to fight for our freedom and to accomplish the mission. It's not about you, it's not about the individual—it's about the mission.

Again, many service members will be physically or mentally exhausted when they return home. They might not have the energy or the desire right away to put into a relationship. They might not be able to meet the minimum standards you expect from a partner. So allow them time to acclimate back to this country and back to living as a civilian in the United States.

There is nothing black or white about what happened to them while serving their country. There are good things that happened while they were deployed and conversely, there are going to be some horrible experiences that are hard for them to share. They often get asked the question, "Hey, did you kill someone?" That is a question that none of them can correctly answer. They might have been in a situation where they acted quickly, but it wasn't quickly enough, and they lost a comrade. Perhaps they were a part of a mission where people were killed but they did not directly pull a trigger, push a button, or give a direct command. You can't assume that they feel a certain sense of vindication, loss, or trauma until they've had a chance to come back to this country and process what happened.

I've suggested that a service member who has been deployed and or been involved in any kind of combat situation allow at least four to six months to process through his or her emotions and assimilate back into everyday living in this country before he or she even considers reconnecting with others in a social dating situation. This will assist all involved in closing the gap between those who had the war experience and those who want to understand it better.

Wright

Are there any common mistakes that you see people make in their relationships?

Coleman

Probably the most common mistake I see people make regarding their relationships is to mistake infatuation for love and fall too far, too fast. There are five stages that every relationship progresses through and the timing of each stage can be different for every person.

Infatuation is the initial stage. It is immediate and demanding. You catch another person's eyes, your heart begins to palpitate, and your palms begin to sweat. In your mind the person can do little wrong because at this stage they are still "perfect."

You then progress to Discovery, during which you start to realize that the person is a human being—one who will make mistakes and have faults. He or she is far from perfect. From there you advance to Reality whereby you know the person well enough to gauge the truth of the entire situation. Who is he or she, really? What are the dreams, goals, abilities, and desires of the person? What are the person's faults? Are the faults deal-breakers for you? Do you feel a true connection to the person? From there, you move on to the Decision stage. Do you move forward or call it quits? If your decision is to cease moving forward, it ends right there. If you decide to move forward, you make a Commitment (the final stage) to one another and then do all that you can to enter into a long-term, healthy, and successful partnership.

There are three types of love people will experience in a healthy relationship. The first type of love is called *eros* love. The word *eros* comes from the Greek and is the root word for the word "erotic," pertaining to sexually based love. It is applicable when people are physically attracted to each other.

Then there's *agape* love, again from the Greek, meaning love that is more spiritual, not sexual in nature. Agape is a heart-felt love that grows stronger over time, and it's a love that you choose—even when the other person isn't being all that lovable!

Finally, there is *philia* love, whereby you sense great friendship and kinship with another person. Philia love is often referred to as "brotherly love" that again grows stronger over time.

So in every quality relationship between two people, you want to have the three types of love. Some people, however, jump too quickly and too deeply into eros love and forsake developing the other types of love. That will not bode well for the future, as no matter how intense physical chemistry is, physical attraction will ultimately wane and without the other loves to rely upon a relationship, is certain to fail.

For women there is another common mistake that I observe. Women have a tendency to remain in relationships far too long out of a sense of obligation. Even though they no longer have feelings for or interest in another person, they stay with him or her, often in an unhappy and unsatisfying relationship. I believe that this occurs for three distinct reasons.

The first reason is called "No Zero Return." I have observed that overwhelmingly women place more investment into relationships than the average man, and they don't want zero return on their investment.

The second reason is called "No Break-Ins," meaning that they don't want to spend the time and effort to "break someone in" and then "give him or her away" to someone else.

And the third and final reason is "The Big Lie." Certain women convince themselves that if they "let go" of the person they are with, no one else will want them. Many other people might be interested in dating them, but they're currently involved with someone who is wrong for them. It takes a pretty courageous woman to come to terms with the fact that she has a lot of life left to live and that she should live it with someone who loves her back and not settle.

Wright

This has been a great conversation, and I really appreciate your taking this time today to answer all of these questions for me and for our readers!

Coleman

You're very welcome, and thanks for including me in this project. I honestly believe that it is going to positively impact many lives, so I'm thrilled to be involved.

About David Coleman...

DAVID COLEMAN, known nationwide as The Dating Doctor™ and "America's Real-Life Hitch," has been honored eleven times as America's National Speaker of the Year. He is a highly sought after speaker, entertainer, emcee, author, leadership trainer, retreat facilitator, and radio and television personality. He has keynoted for some of America's top corporations, and appeared at thousands of colleges and civic groups speaking live to over two million people. David lives by the motto, "Where is it said that learning can't be fun and entertainment can't be life-changing?" In any and every capacity, David Coleman changes lives!

David Coleman
The Dating Doctor
President and CEO
Coleman Productions, Inc.
P.O. Box 235
Loveland, OH 45140
866.328.3762
David@DatingDoctor.com
www.DatingDoctor.com

Chapter Twelve

An interview with...

Shannon Wallis

David Wright (Wright)

We're talking with Shannon Wallis. Shannon is the Global Director of Leadership Programs and responsible for the development of top-tier talent for Microsoft's Sales Marketing and Services Organization. For 15 years, she has specialized in manifesting big ideas through transformational change. She works with her clients to define what they want, take the steps to get it, and release the limiting beliefs that hamper their progress. Prior to her current role, she consulted to and held management positions in Fortune 100 businesses as diverse as Coca-Cola and Universal Studios. Her degrees include an MBA from Duke University and a BS in Human Development and Social Policy from Northwestern University. She is an active member of the National Speakers Association and a highly sought after keynote speaker.

In 2000, Shannon founded Create Your Life, an association designed to help individuals discover their passions and manifest them in their lives. Create Your Life offered them a network of supporters who sustained and encouraged them to achieve their dreams. She was drawn to Microsoft in 2004 after hearing its mission, to enable people and businesses throughout the world to realize their full potential. This interview tells the inspiring story of how Shannon's personal and professional expertise crystallized in one transformational experience – a 500 mile hike across northern Spain.

Six years ago, you walked across northern Spain. Why did you do that?

Shannon Wallis (Wallis)

I think the better question is, "Why would anyone, especially someone who is not an avid hiker, strap on a twenty-pound pack with one change of clothes and two sets of underwear, walk through mountains and wheat fields, in the pouring rain and scorching sun, and then search for lodging, water, and food every day for thirty days?" I had a vision—a calling—that was so compelling, I could not say no. And, it was one of the most significant learning experiences in my life, both personally and professionally because it taught me what it really takes to achieve our dreams and to get to our destinations. It wasn't academic theory written in a book about Change Management. The lessons were real and personal.

Prior to having this vision, I had worked for over ten years in Human Resources consulting, specifically Organizational Change. As a consultant at companies like Watson Wyatt, Cooper's & Lybrand, and Price Waterhouse, I learned the methodology for helping organizations get to their destinations.

There are three phases: First, analyze the current state—what's happening today, what's not working well, what best practices exist. Second, envision the desired future state—consider the best practices, adopt or adapt them, or create something new. Third, implement the vision. Although it's much more involved and takes time, this is the basic approach. I worked with many Fortune 500 companies utilizing it. Projects usually ended with people being "downsized," which most people know is just a fancy term for fired. Knowing this was difficult for me, I focused on the opportunities that could be created in the future because of the changes that were implemented.

After several years of consulting and traveling every week, I burned out. I accepted an internal Organizational Change consulting role with The Coca-Cola Company where I didn't have to downsize people. Instead, I focused on getting the best out of the people already there. I had been working at Coke for two years and was participating in a one-year leadership development program when I received "the call."

During a retreat in June 1999, I had a vision to go to northern Spain to do something spiritual. It wasn't a very clear vision, and I didn't understand it. After the retreat, I flew home to Atlanta, and I said to my husband, "Joe, we're moving to Spain."

He replied, "What?"

I said, "I can't explain it, but I have to go to Spain—northern Spain—to do something spiritual. I think it will be in October."

Joe is a pretty remarkable person. Instead of questioning it or complaining about how it might affect his career at Accenture, he supported me and responded, "Okay." My journey to Santiago had begun.

Two days after returning from the retreat, my manager walked into my office and said, "Shannon, someone from the Madrid office called and asked if you'd be interested in a similar position there."

I jumped out of my chair and started screaming, "I knew it! I knew it! I knew this was going to happen!" I told her about my vision of going to Spain.

"Whoa, hold on a moment!" she responded. "Things at Coke change very quickly so don't get too excited yet." Two days after we had that conversation Coke experienced a crisis in Belgium that changed the entire European business plan and would eventually lead to the CEO's departure. As a result of the change in business, the job in Madrid disappeared.

However, a different position surfaced two months later. I was asked to interview to be the Chief of Staff to the President of Central Europe based in Vienna, Austria. It was a position many people desired, but I thought it was a long shot for me. In fact, when I was first asked to interview, I laughed and said, "Why would I interview for that job? It always goes to a Marketing or Finance person. Why would they take an Org Change consultant?" In the end, there were three final candidates: a person from Corporate Marketing, another from Corporate Finance, and me. Although I told my friends and family that my chances were slim, deep down, I believed the job was mine. I could see myself in the job. I believed that it was a part of my personal purpose in life, and that I was meant to go.

When I walked off the plane in Vienna it was early morning. I hadn't slept and was looking forward to showering and resting before my afternoon interview. I was greeted by a driver who explained that my interview had been rescheduled for that morning because the President had another commitment and needed to travel in the afternoon. "Can you come to the office right away and talk to him?"

I felt brain dead. I hadn't slept, and I was exhausted. I replied, "Of course!"

During the interview, I remember being less than eloquent. I thought to myself, "What are you saying? Pull it together; you make no sense." But somehow, in the midst of my foggy confusion, I must have said all of the right things because a couple of days later they called and offered me the job. It was late September.

Joe left his job, and we moved in the middle of November. It wasn't the right location or timing, but it was closer to Spain, and I knew that I was getting nearer to my vision. Little did I know that I was about to have one of the most significant experiences in my career as an Organizational Change consultant. I was about to learn that change isn't just about the business—it is very personal. Within a couple of weeks of my arriving in Vienna, the CEO, Doug Ivester, resigned. By mid-January, Coke had a new CEO and my new boss, the President of Central Europe, who was not in his political favor, was out of a job.

So there we were. We had just moved to Vienna. My husband was without a job and my job was eliminated when our President was removed. I couldn't help thinking, "What have I done?" I panicked. Joe and I talked about our situation and decided that we didn't want to return to the United States, yet. We decided that we would try to stay in Europe. I only spoke English, so our best option for a job search seemed to be the United Kingdom. In early February, we flew to London to interview with a variety of companies.

Prior to going to London, I talked to my friend Christy, who said, "I think you should interview with our company," and she arranged an interview for me. A few days before the interview, she called me to tell me more about the woman I would interview with. She mentioned that she thought I would find her very interesting and that she had just returned from a sabbatical. When I met her for the interview, I mentioned that Christy had said she had recently returned from a sabbatical and asked what she had done. She replied, "I walked *El Camino de Santiago*." Without understanding what it was, where it was located, or what it was about, my soul cried out, "I'm going to do that!"

And then I asked, "What is the *Camino*?" She described an eight hundred kilometer footpath across northern Spain that starts in the Pyrenees along the border of France and ends in Northwest Spain at Santiago de Compostela—the place believed to be the burial site of Saint James. *Santiago* is Spanish for Saint James. *El Camino de Santiago*—the way of Saint James—is the pilgrimage to Santiago that began one thousand years ago and has been traveled by millions of individuals from all walks of life since then. The modern *Camino* is traveled by approximately 60,000 pilgrims annually. At its height in popularity during the 1400s and 1500s more than half a million traveled it each year.

It was February 2000 and I finally understood my vision. I was going to walk *El Camino de Santiago*. This I knew. Yet many other things would happen in my life before I would actually step onto the path of Saint James and begin the journey to Santiago.

Wright

So if you didn't go right away. What held you back?

Wallis

Life held me back. After our interviews in London, we returned to Vienna and discussed our options. After much consideration, we realized that we didn't really want to go to London. We wanted to go to Spain. Joe is half Spanish and bilingual. He was born in Spain, which we knew would help speed up the process of getting a work visa. We began the job search in Madrid where we had friends. Joe found a job fairly quickly, and we moved to Madrid in September 2000.

During the interim, I helped in the downsizing of the Central European organization. The "coincidence" of hiring an Org Change consultant into the Chief of Staff role was not lost on me. The Vienna office alone was expected to experience a 90 percent downsizing. It was fortuitous to have an Org Change consultant present during that time instead of someone with the Marketing or Finance background. I was able to help people in a time of need and to see the impact of restructuring from a very personal perspective. It was a humbling experience. I learned the hard way that it wasn't just business—it was personal.

Being a part of that type of downsizing was personally challenging and emotionally draining. When we moved to Spain, I decided to take some time off before I jumped into a new organization. I called it my sabbatical time.

It was a good time to embrace the cultural change that I would experience. I grew up in Sioux Falls, South Dakota, a small town in the middle of the wheat and corn fields and in a family "blessed" with gifts that keep on giving—alcoholism, depression, abandonment, and poverty. Understandably, I dreamed of living a different life. Moving to Vienna and Madrid was, in many respects, like winning the lottery.

My life as an expatriate was completely different from the one of my childhood. I wanted to fully embrace it. I didn't have the opportunity in Vienna because we weren't there very long and I was busy at work. I did have the chance in Madrid. I had struggled to put myself through college and graduate school and then worked like a fiend to be given incredible opportunities in my career. I wanted a break. I wanted to live a little, learn a new language, see the country, and spend time with friends. Now, I had the opportunity. During our first nine months in Madrid, we had nearly sixty visitors.

Our first visitor was Susan, a friend of mine from my MBA program at Duke. She had studied in Spain when she was in college. One day in September, as we were driving around southern Spain, I told her about my vision of walking the *Camino*. Susan had studied in Santiago and had seen the pilgrims on their way to the cathedral. She replied, "When you go, let me know; I'd like to go too." I promised to contact her when I was ready.

While I guided our visitors through Spain and took Spanish lessons, Joe began his new role as a director with a large multi-national consulting firm. By January 2001, it was clear that the job wasn't what he had expected. In fact, my husband, the Marine Reservist, who I jokingly told people was so tough that he could sleep in the dirt and eat dirt, was miserable. In the years I had known him, I had never heard him complain, so I knew it was serious. He left the consulting firm and accepted a position as the European representative with a U.S. based executive search firm with whom he had a prior relationship. The job was 100 percent commission. I was nervous about that, but we had saved my Coca-Cola severance package and had a small cushion while the business was launched in Europe.

For the first three months, he traveled and built relationships with organizations, but he did not earn any money. This was expected because it normally takes three months in the United States to see a return on investment. We thought that it might take a few more months in Europe. Then we learned that I was pregnant. We were thrilled about the pregnancy, yet nervous about the lack of income to support ourselves and the baby. Instead of giving up, we decided to give the organizational relationships a little more time to bear fruit. At that point, Joe could manage the relationships remotely, so he decided to take a three-month Marine Reserve assignment at Camp LeJeune in the United States. It would provide regular income and give us a little more time to figure out our next step—stay in Europe with the new job or return to the United States and find employment there.

Joe left for Camp LeJeune in mid-June 2001 right after I had completed my first trimester. He would be gone during my second trimester but we weren't concerned because I had already passed the first. The day he left, I had a doctor's appointment scheduled. While Joe was en route to the United States, the doctor said in Spanish, "Shannon, I'm very sorry; I can't find the heartbeat." Because my Spanish was not perfect, I hoped that I had misunderstood. I hadn't. In fact, I learned that I had probably miscarried three weeks earlier. I was devastated and felt terribly alone as the doctor described the procedure and hospital stay that were required. I had no way of immediately contacting Joe, which added to my feeling of isolation. By the time I could talk to him, I could barely speak.

The remainder of the summer was very difficult for me, but as mid-September approached, I looked forward to Joe's return. Then 9/11 happened. Joe was still on active duty at the time. As a communications officer, he was mobilized to Stuttgart, Germany, where the satellite systems are monitored. Our decision to stay or go was on hold.

Prior to arriving at Stuttgart, we were able to spend a couple of weeks together at home in Madrid, and I was blessed to get pregnant again. I was thrilled. Even though Joe wasn't there, I had something to look forward to and my doctor seemed quite certain that I would be fine. A couple of months passed, my pregnancy progressed normally, and my doctor said it was okay for me to travel to Houston for the birth of my sister's first child. Because of my history, he asked me to see a doctor while I was in the United States but assured me that he didn't expect any complications. When I arrived, my sister delivered her baby and the next day I went to the doctor to discover that I had miscarried again. During this difficult time, I was grateful to have the support of my sister, but it was bittersweet with a new nephew at home.

I returned to Madrid and saw my husband over the holidays. On New Year's Eve, as we toasted the New Year, my husband said solemnly, "Shannon, it was a tough year, but it's over and it can't get any worse." As soon as he said that, my stomach turned over and I thought, "Oh no, something really bad is coming." A few days later, my mother called and told me she had cancer. My first thought was, "No way, this can't be happening. I've lost my job, my husband is gone, I've had two miscarriages, and now my mother has cancer." My mother is my rock. Through all of the tough times in my family, she hung in there. I started to cry and she said, "Don't worry, the doctor says it isn't that bad; it's only Stage 1."

I flew to the United States to help my mother recover from her surgery. We didn't expect that she would need chemotherapy or radiation, but we knew that she would be off her feet for a few weeks. So, I flew from Madrid to Seattle and they performed the surgery. We then discovered it wasn't Stage 1—it was Stage 4 and the cancer had metastasized to her lymph nodes and rib cage. A short surgical recovery turned into months of chemotherapy and radiation. When the majority of the treatments were completed in May, I returned home emotionally and physically exhausted. Joe was still in Stuttgart but expected to end his assignment in a few weeks.

Around this time I started to read the many books I had collected about the *Camino*. When Joe arrived home, he noticed the pile on my side of the bed. He looked at the books and he looked at me and asked, "Are you going to do the *Camino* now?" I stared at him, paralyzed, as the following thoughts went through my head in a millisecond, "Why am I reading these books? Am I going to walk the *Camino?* How can I go at this time? We've been separated for nearly a year? It's been a terrible year. We should be together now. We should be starting our family." Without waiting for my response, he said, "You should do the *Camino*. I want you to go." In that moment my first two lessons from the *Camino* arrived.

Wright

What were they?

Wallis

Know Where You are Going (number one) and *Know What You are Leaving Behind (number two)*.

Until that point, the *Camino* had been nothing more than a romantic vision—a calling that I couldn't explain. At that moment, it became a symbol for a new beginning. After the loss, pain, and fear of the prior year and a half, I was exhausted emotionally and expecting the worst to happen. I wanted to put it behind me. I didn't understand how the *Camino* was going to help that, but I was absolutely certain that whatever it offered was going to be better than what I was sitting in emotionally at that point in time. I was conscious that I needed to let go of some things to move forward in my life.

Wright

Shannon, how do these lessons help us get to the destination?

Wallis

First, you need to know what you really want. Most of us wander aimlessly in life bumping into things that sometimes work for us. But when we know what we want in life, our actions can be much more prescriptive. Imagine the difference in planning a vacation when you say, I want to see the volcanoes of Costa Rica versus, I'd like to go somewhere warm. Clarity makes taking action easier.

Second, you need to know why you are making the change. Most people resist change. Understanding why we want to make a change provides momentum for moving forward. It doesn't have to be as extreme as the pain I felt. It could be as simple as, "This job is no longer satisfying to me and I'm not learning anymore."

As I made the decision to go, Susan's voice echoed in my head, "When you go, let me know; I'd like to go, too." Yet, I hesitated. Susan had started a new job three months earlier and I doubted that she could come. But it ate at me. I sent her an e-mail with two sentences: "I am leaving for the *Camino* in two weeks. Do you want to come?" She sent an e-mail to me the next day. "Funny you should ask, I just lost my job. I'm coming."

So, my third lesson was, *Invite Others to Participate, They Might Surprise You (number three)*. Tell people about your plans to do something different, to go to a new destination. Say, "I want a different job or career," "I want to lose fifty pounds," "I want to run a marathon." Whatever it is, we are less likely to back out when someone not only encourages us, but also agrees to accompany us in our journey. Furthermore, our supporters may have hidden talents or connections that will help us arrive at our destination, thus our probability of success increases.

Two weeks later Susan arrived in Madrid. Given the circumstances in our lives, we had decided that we would only walk for about two weeks. A lot of people walk the length of the *Camino* a week at a time. They start in one place, walk for a week, and return the following year to pick up where they left off. That was our plan. We had our packs and walking sticks—everything that we needed for our journey.

The next morning we were on a train that would take us to Pamplona, the closest city to Roncesvalles we could get to by train. Roncesvalles is the town on the border of France and Spain where the *Camino* originates. We arrived in Pamplona around ten in the morning to discover that the bus to Roncesvalles did not leave until much later in the afternoon.

We were much too excited to wait for the bus. Realizing that it was only forty-four kilometers (twenty-seven miles) east to Roncesvalles and being from the city, we hailed a taxi. Ironically, we traveled east to Roncesvalles so that we could walk west and return to Pamplona a few days later.

Winding through the mountains, a shocking revelation hit me and I blurted out to Susan, "It's a long way to Pamplona."

She replied, "You're just getting that?"

What I meant was, "What was I thinking? The cab ride is taking forever and the first thing we have to do is walk back to Pamplona. Am I kidding myself? I'm going to walk to Pamplona with twenty pounds on my back? This is crazy." I thought of quitting right then and there. Many journeys end before the first step is taken, so people never get to their destinations.

The next lesson of the *Camino* hit me like a ton of bricks. *It's a Long Way to Pamplona—Every Journey Begins with the First Step (number four)*. Many times when we look at the destination, we feel overwhelmed. The journey seems too long. It is a guarantee that we will never arrive at the destination if we don't take the first step. Getting to Pamplona is critical because it is a milestone that moves us in the right direction. If we can get to Pamplona—the first milestone—we are that much closer to our destination.

When we arrived in Roncesvalles, the Pilgrim Center at the church was closed. At the Center, we intended to collect our Pilgrim's Passports—documents pilgrims carry that serve as proof of the journey when they arrive in Santiago and request the certificate for completing the *Camino*. In addition, passports are required to obtain lodging at *refugios*—refuge places with beds, showers, and kitchens for pilgrims. A *refugio* is the rustic equivalent of a dormitory. It provides the basics. Hot water is a bonus. As pilgrims walk the *Camino* each day, they search for shelter at night in a *refugio*. Each *refugio* has a unique seal that is stamped on the passport and the passport becomes a record of the journey.

As we waited for the Center to open, we talked to other *peregrinos* (pilgrims). We met two Canadians, Christine and Judy. For some reason, I believe that all Canadians are outdoorsy and avid hikers. Their packs were twice the size of ours and contained the latest and greatest hiking gear. As they displayed their gear and talked about the best way to wear your pack, I became concerned. They seemed so knowledgeable. I wondered if we were ready for the *Camino*. I had my answer the next day when I saw Christine and Judy struggling with their packs along the road. Within a few days, they had packed up half their gear and mailed it to Santiago to pick up when they completed their journey.

The next lesson of the *Camino* had arrived, *Pack Light (number five)*. Many of us have had the experience of thinking we have finally figured out all of the rules to win the game only to learn that the rules, or some of them, have changed. We can't assume that what has gotten us to where we are today—our skills, beliefs, and assumptions—will move us to where we want to be in the future. To get to our destinations, we must discard some of the things that made us successful in the past to create room to build new capability that gives us a higher chance of success.

The Center also had a *refugio*. After it opened, we began the ritual that would be ours for the remainder of our journey. We found a bed, unpacked, showered, and then searched for dinner. On that first day, we did not need to wash our clothes. In most *refugios*, pilgrims cook their meals with others. In Roncesvalles—the starting place—pilgrims dine together in a small café.

From the moment we began to unpack, the questions began. "Where are you from?" "Are you going to Santiago?" As I mentioned earlier, Susan and I didn't plan to go to Santiago. We were going as far as we could in the next two weeks. But as the other pilgrims asked me, "Are you going to Santiago?" my soul responded as it had done when I first heard of the *Camino*. "*Yes, I am going to Santiago!*" But my head said, "No, that wasn't the agreement. I told Joe that I am only going for two weeks." He had just returned; I couldn't be gone for a month. Besides, Susan had to get back to start her job search and we were now in this together.

However, the next morning Susan said to me, "I just want you to know that I've decided to go to Santiago." I responded, "Me, too!" At that moment, we committed to a more specific destination. It was no longer just about the *Camino*—it was about Getting to Santiago!

The next lesson was clear: *Commit to Going and Go! (number six).* Too many times when we look at our destination, we get stuck. The distance seems too far, the work required to get there too great. We wonder whether we should stay or go. We give this stuck place a lot of terms like, sitting on the fence, limbo, or the neutral zone. Whatever we call it, staying stuck is as much of a decision as deciding to move forward. Mentally commit and get off the fence. Say, "I'm going to Santiago." Without commitment to the destination, our chances of success are limited.

Susan and I started walking to Pamplona that morning on our way to Santiago. The first couple of days were really fun. Susan and I hadn't seen each other in over a year and we caught up on each other's lives. But, after the second day, I noticed that matching Susan's stride was difficult for me. Susan is eight inches taller than I—all in her legs. At five feet, my legs were too short to match her stride. Likewise, it was just as difficult for Susan to slow down and take shorter strides. During a normal hike, it would not have been an issue. But we realized that continuing to walk together eight hours per day with twenty pounds on our backs for another thirty days would be painful. We were initially saddened by this discovery because we had looked forward to walking together. But even though we realized that we would have to walk separately, each at her own pace, we still agreed to get to Santiago together.

It was an important lesson—*Everyone Walks at a Different Pace, Work With It (number seven).* As we move toward our destinations, some of the people who agree to join us may take a different approach to getting there. We all have our own pace and it is important to respect the differences and figure out ways to work with them.

Wright

I know that you arrived in Santiago together, how did you manage to do that if you were walking separately?

Wallis

Susan and I agreed quickly to some guiding principles that helped us to "walk together" while walking separately. If we hadn't agreed to them, it would have been very easy to get separated because we could have easily stopped at different towns or *refugios* along the way and ended up days apart.

Three things helped us: First, every night before bed, we looked at our map and planned the next day. We agreed on the town and *refugio* to meet in. We agreed that no matter how tired we were, even if we thought we couldn't continue on, we would get to that location. We trusted each other to follow through on that agreement. We knew that if we didn't, we would get separated. Second, we communicated a lot. When we woke up in the morning, we checked in with each other and reminded each other of the agreed destination for the day.

Then we had a ritual of a morning coffee. At the first town with an open café, Susan would stop to have a coffee and wait for me to arrive. Even though I would leave before she did in the morning, she would have her coffee first. By the time I would arrive, she was ready to move on. We'd check in with how each other was doing, offer each other *"¡Buen Camino!"* (the greeting of pilgrims on the *Camino*, which means "Good Journey!") and she would be on her way as I sat down for my coffee. That was how we stayed connected.

Third, we followed the *flechas amarillas*—yellow arrows. The yellow arrows are the markers along the *Camino* that point you in the direction toward Santiago and let you know that you are still on the right path. Some of the arrows are obvious while others are not. I got lost once and had to backtrack one hour to find the right marker. I learned that if I didn't see an arrow every couple of hours, I had better head back to the last marker I had seen.

The *Camino* taught me that to get to the destination, you have to *Agree on Your Milestones (number eight), Communicate, Communicate, and Communicate Again (number nine), and Find the Yellow Arrows and Move Forward (number ten).* When moving toward our destinations, it's important to set small goals for ourselves that are achievable. I tell my clients, baby steps become journeys. Ask yourself, "What am I going to do today to move myself in the right direction?" Tell everyone you know about the milestones. It helps to maintain focus and motivation when they are achieved. Finally, look for the signs or markers that you are moving in the right direction. If we are honest with ourselves, we see them but choose to ignore them. Down deep, most of us know when it is time to move to our next destination. We choose not to. We can just as easily choose to pay attention and follow the markers.

Before I share the last five lessons, I want to explain my daily *Camino* experience. I woke up every morning at five and the first thing I did was take an ibuprofen. I did this to prepare my feet, which was painful work. You would not want to have seen my feet. On the second day when my first blister arrived, the *hospitalera* (the person who runs the *refugio)* said, "Don't worry. You'll only have that for a couple of days." I was actually kind of proud of that first blister. I thought, "Yea! Now I'm a pilgrim. I have the blister to prove it." On the fourth day, I had three or four blisters. The *hospitalera* said, "One week, maximum! I've never seen anyone who has had blisters beyond one week." I quickly learned that I was going to be the exception to the rule. By the time I reached Santiago I had sixteen blisters on my feet! All were in various stages of disintegration or healing. I was famous on the *Camino*. I would arrive in *refugios* and *hospitaleros* would say, "I've heard of you! You're the American with the blisters."

There were times when I would stand up and want to pass out from the shooting pains that went through my body because of the blisters. Every morning started with ibuprofen. Then I would prepare my feet. I had to wash them, drain the blisters with needle and thread, put antiseptic on them and then gauze and tape them. Then I would have a light breakfast, check my map, and remember where I planned to meet Susan. When I stopped for coffee, I would check my feet to let them air a little bit.

I was careful about my feet because a simple infection can lead to blood infection and if a *hospitalera* find outs and a doctor learns of it, the *Camino* is over for you. Pilgrims with seemingly minor health issues are often sent home because people have died on the *Camino* from infection and other things. Therefore, I knew to be diligent about my feet. In fact, I learned so much about healing feet that I became the healer of others. (Sadly, my foot healing skills aren't valued in my current profession.)

After my coffee, I walked and walked and walked until I arrived at the agreed *refugio*. I would find the bed that Susan had saved for me when she arrived. If I hadn't invited Susan, I would have slept on the floor most nights! Inviting others pays off in unexpected ways. Each evening I would shower, wash my clothes, prepare my feet, get lunch, shop for that night's dinner and the next day's breakfast, rest, and make dinner with friends. Around 8:00 PM, I would pop in my ear plugs to eliminate others' snoring and go to sleep.

By the tenth day of the *Camino* I had easily mastered the routine as I was entering Burgos, the place I was going to meet Joe. Shortly after I made the decision to go to Santiago, I called Joe to let him know. He was very supportive and agreed to meet me in Burgos. He drove to Burgos from Madrid in about two hours. Seeking sympathy, I showed my damaged feet to Joe. I told him about the trials of the *Camino* and how I walked in spite of the pain, the rain, and the lightning storms that we had experienced that morning. I explained what it meant to be a pilgrim and that I had done this every day. *Every day!* I wanted him to agree that I was indeed brave for carrying on in spite of it all.

My Marine looked at me and said, "What were you thinking? It wouldn't be a pilgrimage if it weren't challenging."

What did he just say? This was not the response I was looking for. I was so *mad!* I couldn't believe he said that to me. I thought, "He doesn't understand what this is all about!" I was so angry! The next day after he left, I told Susan and my new friend, Lori, about his insensitivity. I said in a sing songy voice, "It wouldn't be a pilgrimage if it weren't challenging." They were as outraged as I was. Clearly he did not understand! We talked about his comment for not only several kilometers, but several days! But, it was interesting because the more we talked about it the more it become a mantra when something wasn't going quite as easily as we hoped— "Well, you know, it wouldn't be a pilgrimage if it weren't challenging." When we met pilgrims along the *Camino* who had their own stories of woe, we would nod and say "Well it wouldn't be a pilgrimage if it weren't challenging!"

In truth, my husband, the Marine, understood better than any of us. *It Wouldn't Be a Pilgrimage If It Weren't Challenging (number eleven).* If you think getting to the destination is going to be easy, think again. Change is seldom easy. We can pick the destination and follow the markers but it won't be a piece of cake. That's why all of the other lessons are so important. We need them to help keep us on the path so we don't give up.

Leaving Burgos we entered what would become the most challenging stretch of the *Camino* for me. The distance between Burgos and Leon was flat, hot, and covered as far as the eye could see with wheat fields. It would take ten days to walk the distance before we reached the foothills of Galicia. Being from South Dakota, I knew wheat fields. By this time, I had at least twelve of the sixteen blisters. I was in a lot of pain and I was alone. Being of fairly average height, Susan usually walked with others. I, on the other hand, walked alone because my stride was shorter and my pace was slower than average. The wheat fields drew me right into my childhood, which, as you can probably guess, was less than ideal. I spent most of my childhood ashamed of my family situation and trying to hide it from my friends. For the better part of my childhood, my father was an active alcoholic or absent from the home. My mother suffered from clinical depression but she managed to work and keep food on the table. We had very little besides each other. I was the oldest child who filled in the parental gaps. As I walked between Burgos and Leon, I was stuck in the mire of it all. I could not escape it.

Then, the *Day of Devils* arrived. It is a distance of over twenty kilometers during which pilgrims walk with little access to shade and no access to well water. This was a particularly bad day for me.

On the *Day of Devils*, I was contemplating the three things all pilgrims hear when traveling the *Camino*. First, the *Camino* calls you. I absolutely believe that. Second, everyone's *Camino* is different. I was living that. From my perspective that day, Susan was having a jolly time with her walking companions. Third, the *Camino* is a metaphor for life. If that was true—my life was about pain and being alone. I didn't like the implications. I was at my lowest point emotionally. I was in terrible pain that day—it was very hot and I felt horribly alone. I looked in front of me and saw nothing and nobody. I looked behind me and saw nothing and nobody, except the wheat fields, for what seemed like miles. I felt so hurt and angry. I was particularly mad at God for allowing this pain in my life. I felt sorry for myself. I shook my walking stick wildly at the heavens and screamed. I pounded it on the ground multiple times with all of my force and cried, "If the *Camino* is a metaphor for life, why is my life so filled with pain?" I cried, screamed, and doubled over in pain thinking that if I gave up now, no one would even find me until the next day because I was usually the last one to arrive. I truly considered giving up, and in some ways I did because I finally surrendered and said, "I just can't do this, God, because if this is the way it's going to be, if I am going to be alone through all of this pain, well, I just don't want to think about it anymore. I can't do it." But, I was resolved to my fate.

At this moment of surrender, I heard, *"¡Buen Camino!"* I froze. I thought I was hallucinating because I had just looked behind me and had not seen anyone for miles. I was jolted out of my frenzy and started to walk again. A few steps later, again I heard, *"¡Buen Camino!"* I still had tears running down my face and I was shaking and I thought, "No, I am hallucinating because of the heat." But as I thought this, I slowly turned around and several meters behind me I saw an older woman approaching me. I had seen her a few times in the past few days. She was in her sixties and she kept to herself. She was moving quickly.

My mind was racing, "Where did she come from? Did she see my wild display? She had to have seen me. This is so humiliating." As she approached me, she again offered, *"¡Buen Camino!"* I was so embarrassed I could barely make eye contact. I motioned for her to pass me, because everybody passed me on the *Camino*. Nobody walked at my pace. But she slowed down to walk with me. I thought, "Of all days, someone wants to walk with me."

Again she said, *"¡Buen Camino!"* softly this time. I thought, disgustedly, "Yeah! *¡Buen Camino!* all right." Instead I said to her, "You know, I am ready to die."

She looked at me and said, "It's not your day to die."

I looked at her quizzically and said, "What?"

She pointed to a marker on the road. Markers are placed on the *Camino* where pilgrims have died. They are not common, but they are occasional reminders that not everybody makes it. She pointed to the marker and said, "It was his day to die. It is not your day to die for I am here to walk with you."

I started to cry. I knew in that moment that God had been with me—I had never been alone.

We walked together—this beautiful older woman, whom I had avoided at the *refugios* because she seemed strange—and me. She had an incredible dark sense of humor. She told me stories and made me laugh for the next two hours.

I asked her, "Why are you walking with me? No one walks with me."

"Every day I get up and I look for the person who needs me," she replied, "and I knew today was your day—that you would need me."

I was stunned. I thought she was an amazing woman and wondered how she knew because she was right. She was from Germany. I don't know what happened to her. But I do believe that God worked through her. And I believe that I was never alone.

Wright

Shannon, it seems like there are so many things you could have learned from that. What was the lesson for you?

Wallis

Support Comes When You Least Expect It and From the Most Unlikely Places (number twelve). All journeys to the destination will have moments of despair. I suspect that the level of despair varies by how difficult the journey is. In those moments when we think we cannot go one step further and we are truly ready to give up, we must have faith that the support we need will materialize. Since then, I have seen that assistance show up for many people and organizations.

From that moment forward my *Camino* experience changed. I accepted it as it was meant to be. I decided that although my *Camino* was different from others', it was no longer going to be the one focused on pain.

The next morning when I got up I still had physical pain, and as was the custom, other pilgrims asked how my feet were doing because, again, I was a bit of a novelty. Instead of sharing the details of how many blisters I had and how I cared for them, I simply answered that they were fine and I'd like to talk about something else. I decided that I didn't have to share my pain with everyone. I decided to enjoy what was going on around me, and I walked on to the next town.

In the next *refugio*, the *hospitalera*, Laura, looked at my feet while I was cleaning them in the courtyard and asked, "What's wrong with your feet?"

"Nothing's wrong with my feet," I replied. I was on my new path.

She looked at me strangely and said, "No, something is wrong with your feet."

I thanked her and explained that I was fine.

She looked at me firmly and said, "No. Something's wrong with your feet. I've walked the *Camino* three times. Something's wrong with your feet. Come with me."

I felt conflicted and hesitated. I had found courage and peace in accepting my fate. It was strange to have come to terms with it only to think a respite might be near. Laura did not budge. She told me to pick up my boots and follow her.

She escorted me to the cobbler who looked at my boots and informed me that the insoles were the wrong size. He showed me how the heel of my foot was coming down on the insole incorrectly. He immediately created new ones for me. I had to admit that they felt better.

Next, Laura took me to the pharmacist who looked at my feet and explained that I was allergic to the tape that held the gauze patches in place. It turned out that the red, bumpy, scaly, itchy patches around the blisters were a rash generated by the allergy. She gave me some cream and a special, hypoallergenic tape. Finally, Laura escorted me back to her office at the *refugio* where she handed me two of the largest sanitary napkins I had ever seen. I politely declined explaining that I did not need them.

She said, "No, they're for your sandals. Part of your problem is that your feet aren't getting enough air. Remove the adhesive on the bottom of the pad, put them on the base of the sandal, and step into the sandal with the cotton facing up. Try it."

I did as I was told, and it was—*heaven! Heaven!* It felt as though I was walking on marshmallows. Prior to that moment, I would prepare my feet and then put on my sandals when I arrived at the *refugio*. My friends would laugh because I would walk hunched over like an old lady because my feet were in so much pain that I could barely stand up. With this innovation, I was prancing down the street, so happy in my sandals cushioned with sanitary napkins.

I learned a great lesson that day about getting to the destination, *Innovate (number thirteen)*. Look for ideas that are outside of your comfort zone. I felt pretty silly the first time I put those sanitary napkins in my sandals. Afterward, I felt so good that I didn't care what anybody else thought. "Oh, there's that strange American with the blisters and the sanitary napkin sandals." Well, as noted earlier, we can't always count on the things that got us to our current destination to get us to the next. We have to talk with people we don't normally talk with and try things that seem out of the ordinary. We need to read something new and different; we never know where the next idea or connection will come from that will move us one step closer to our destinations.

After meeting Laura, I felt better. I wasn't in as much pain. Interestingly, this is when my *Camino* experience really started to change. To receive a certificate for completing the *Camino*, a pilgrim must walk one hundred kilometers (about sixty miles) of the path.

Susan and I had walked a little over four hundred miles when kids started showing up along the path. In the summer, high schools drop off busloads of teenagers along the *Camino* so they can walk the last one hundred kilometers, pick up their certificate, and have something noteworthy to put on their resumes. The *Camino* becomes one big *fiesta*.

We went from a tranquil, reflective *Camino* to "party time." But, more annoyingly, they stole our trick. Having boundless energy, the *niños* (children, as we called them) would send a sprinter ahead to grab the beds. The "real" pilgrims, Susan, Lori, and those who had started in Roncesvalles, would arrive and the beds would be gone. We would either sleep on the floor or walk on to the next city hoping that other *niños* had not captured those beds too. It was frustrating but we kept our humor by adding lines to Susan's new poem, *¡Niños, niños, porqué hay niños?* Children, children, why are they here? We wished that they would go away.

But they didn't go away, and we adapted. We learned to ask the *niños* where they thought they might end up that day and walk to a different location. We spoke to the *hospitaleros* who, having walked the *Camino*, understood our plight and would try to find us the quietest space in the *refugio*, occasionally offering us their private rooms. I learned, *Niños, niños, porqué hay niños? . . . Why not?* (number fourteen). All journeys involve nuisances along the road. By accepting them, whatever they may be, we can all get to the destination, regardless of our differing intentions. The road needs to be wide enough for all people to reach the destination and wider still so that we can give way to those who might upset us along the way. After all, the *Camino* is different for everybody.

We arrived in Santiago and went immediately to the cathedral. For most pilgrims, this is where their *Camino* ends. My *Camino* was not yet finished. I started to cry. I fell down in the cathedral. I was so grateful to be there, but I knew it was not yet complete for me. I told my friends along the *Camino* that it was my

3G *Camino*. Three Generations. I walked the *Camino* for my mother, myself, and my future generations.

I did not tell them that along the path, I carried the ultrasounds of the two children that I had miscarried. I did not know how to throw them away. For months they had sat on my desk at home because I didn't know what to do with them. At the cathedral, I wrote a letter to St. James. I put their pictures with the letter and I turned their souls over to the care of St. James. I explained that I couldn't carry them with me anymore. If I wanted to truly arrive at the destination, I had to let go of them. I then placed the letter and their pictures in a box at the cathedral. As soon as I did that, I had the most incredible feeling of Hope. I didn't even know that I had lost it. I knew I had been very, very sad, but I didn't know that hope had vanished. In the moment that I let them go, hope returned for me. I knew that I would return to Madrid and that I would have a family. I had arrived in "Santiago." I had arrived at *my* destination.

Although our "Santiagos" are different, getting to the destination is possible for all of us if we heed the *Camino's* lessons. I did get to Santiago. Today, I have a mother who has been free of cancer for five years. I have a wonderful husband who has supported me in every journey I have taken since then. And, I have two beautiful daughters, Savannah and Fiona. Ultimately, I learned to *Count Your Blessings—Not Your Blisters (number fifteen)*.

¡Buen Camino!

About Shannon Wallis...

SHANNON WALLIS is the Director of Worldwide Leadership Programs for Microsoft's Sales Marketing and Services Group. She is an executive coach, consultant, and teacher with twenty years of international work experience in leadership development and organizational change. Prior to her current role, she consulted to and held management positions in Fortune 100 businesses as diverse as Coca-Cola, Universal Studios, and Microsoft. Her degrees include an MBA from Duke University and a BS in Human Development and Social Policy from Northwestern University. She is an active member of the National Speakers Association.

In 2002, she completed El Camino de Santiago, a 500-mile walking pilgrimage across northern Spain. Her keynote address, "Getting to the Destination: 15 Lessons from The Camino," is popular with individuals and organizations embarking on major change.

Shannon Wallis
Microsoft
425.457.4707
swallis@microsoft.com
www.theyellowarrow.com

Chapter Thirteen

An interview with...

Bob DeMers

David Wright (Wright)

Today we are talking with Bob DeMers, the founder and principal of Coaching Works, a relationship-driven and results-orientated coaching, consulting, organizational, and leadership development firm in Charlotte, North Carolina. As a Certified Professional Coach, Certified Mediator, Licensed Clinical Professional Counselor (LCPC), Licensed Alcohol and Drug Counselor (LADC), former television meteorologist, and long-term business owner, he brings a wide-range of professional expertise and life experience in helping his clients elevate their levels of personal, professional, relational, and business success. Bob is an active member of the Charlotte Chamber of Commerce, Lake Norman Chamber of Commerce, International Coach Federation, Charlotte Area Chapter of International Coach Federation, Charlotte Area Chapter of the Society of Human Resource Management, and Rotary International.

Being passionate about a great many things, including his family, music, weather, the Boston Red Sox, and sharing the best of what he's learned about life with others, Bob is currently authoring the first in a series of books, *Emotional Composting 101*, a practical, insightful, and intriguingly quantum perspective on emotions and how to effectively harness and leverage this powerfully creative energy toward achieving personal, professional, relational, and business success.

Bob, welcome to *Blueprint for Success!*

Bob DeMers (DeMers)

Thank you very much, David!

Wright

I'm intrigued by the sound of "Emotional Composting." What exactly is it?

DeMers

Let me share with you a delightful, yet powerful example of emotional composting in action, and then expand on its meaning from there.

Last Valentine's Day, my wife and I surprised our then eight-year-old daughter with some treats from the Valentine's Day "Fairy," which she found on the kitchen table during breakfast. Included was a very sweet note written by the Valentine's Fairy herself (my left hand), which caught my daughter's eye. She said it looked a lot like the notes written by the Easter Bunny and Santa Claus, and asked if I'd written it. My wife squirmed uncomfortably, not wanting me to blow Santa's cover. Knowing that I was busted, I had no choice but to fess up.

As you can imagine, my daughter became quite upset. As my wife and I listened appreciatively, she vented her feelings of anger, betrayal, and sadness, letting us know directly that she didn't appreciate having been lied to. After a short while, she became quiet and started out the door toward school.

As she stepped outside, she turned to me and said, "If you give me eight dollars—one dollar for every year that you and Mom lied to me about Santa—we'll be even."

Talk about an effective emotional management strategy! She leveraged her angst about being lied to and the loss of the magic of Santa (not to mention the Easter Bunny and the Valentine's Fairy) into a positive cash flow opportunity!

Although only eight years old at the time, my daughter's example speaks marvelously to the heart of what emotional composting is—the process of openly, honestly, and effectively identifying, acknowledging, and expressing one's feelings, and leveraging this powerfully transformative information and energy toward one's best interests and the greater good of all concerned.

In other words, emotional composting recycles the most nutritious elements of emotional experience into a rich and fertile "emotional compost" (improved awareness, perspective, focus, insight, clarity, trust, wisdom, vision, creativity, innovation, passion, opportunity, etc.). This can be leveraged toward future personal, relational, professional, and/or business success in much the same way that organic composting leverages the most nutritious elements of discarded organic remains toward the success of future plant growth.

As such, emotional composting is a form of biomimicry in which an efficient, practical, and powerful process naturally occurring in Mother Nature is replicated by humankind, in this instance, emotions being composted and recycled within the framework of human relationships. To appreciate the significance of what we are talking about, however, it is essential to have a basic understanding of the processes involved with organic composting.

Wright

What would the reader need to know about organic composting in order to understand the processes driving emotional composting?

DeMers

Here are some key points to keep in mind: The definition of "organic" in this context means being derived from something that is or once was living (e.g., an apple from a tree, grass clippings, or plant remains). All organic material is governed by the laws of nature, consequently, it eventually decomposes and is recycled back into the grand scheme of things so that new life can spring forth. Organic composting is just a controlled, hands-on approach of decomposing organic material.

The final product of organic composting is humus, more commonly known as compost. This rich, fragrant, and fertile material can be recycled right back into the soil, promoting vigorous plant growth wherever it is applied.

There are two primary methods used to create compost—aerobic composting, in which oxygen is present (an open environment), and anaerobic composting, in which no oxygen is present (a closed environment). Aerobic composting is more labor intensive, requiring aeration of the compost pile at regular intervals in order to maintain maximum aerobic efficiency. Anaerobic composting doesn't require oxygen; as a result, little if any effort is needed to further the process along.

Because it is a hands-on process, aerobic composting is much faster and far less odiferous than anaerobic composing. In fact, organic material composting under airtight conditions will become extremely noxious and may take many years (or longer) to compost. The same material left in an aerated, well-tended composting bin will not be nearly as foul smelling and will take only from a few weeks to a few months to become compost. This is a huge difference in composting efficiency!

Wright

It sure sounds like it! But how does this relate to emotions?

DeMers

To help make this connection, let's highlight some important information about the nature of emotions. Emotions are:

- Energy in flow (E-motion)
- Neither good nor bad in of themselves, although they can certainly feel good or bad, and be labeled and judged this way
- Golden nuggets of truth (even if we don't understand what our emotions are telling us, our emotions don't lie, although we can lie about what we're feeling)
- Rich informational sources (emotional pathways in the brain can process information up to one hundred times faster than cognitive pathways. As brilliant as our thoughts might be, they are still only "dial-up" when compared to the "DSL" processing speed of our emotions)
- Bring our experiences to life (if a picture is worth a thousand words, then an emotion is worth a thousand pictures)

- Quantum gateways to possibility (invisible, alive with potential, and when honestly and effectively put out on the table, can lead to an infinite number of outcomes, none of which are fully predictable beforehand)
- Organic in nature (they're derived from a living organism—ourselves)

This last point is especially important because it provides a powerful basis as to how and why emotions can either help to drive or derail personal, relational, professional, and/or business success when applied to this emotional composting model.

Wright

How so?

DeMers

In the same vein that solid organic material decomposes with time, so do emotions. Even though we can't see this process in action, if we're attentive enough, we'll feel it in action. Again, there are two primary pathways to do this. *Aerobic* emotional composting occurs when emotions are identified, acknowledged, accepted, and expressed openly, honestly, and effectively in the here and now. This reflects an "oxygenated" or open relationship with self and/or others. As with aerobic composting, aerobic emotional composting more quickly and easily generates emotional compost (awareness, insight, clarity, perspective, wisdom, opportunity, etc.), which can then be reinvested and leveraged toward personal, relational, professional, and business growth and success.

When this reinvestment occurs in the moment (something we're naturally able to do as children), it's called being emotionally present. This is an empowering, enlightening, creative, and in some instances, transcendent experience where one becomes more fully aware, engaged, and alive in the here and now. This naturally leads to new perspectives, possibilities, and opportunities not otherwise recognizable when out of tune with one's emotions. Remembering that emotions are loaded with information, this also provides a powerful basis for learning from one's past mistakes and experiences.

For example, a business-coaching client recently acknowledged brooding feelings of stress, frustration, resentment, and disappointment stemming from a long-term relationship with a group of business associates. Once she aired out her feelings and concerns, she gained clarity and perspective, identified unreciprocated loyalties within the relationship, and leveraged this information toward redefining the rules of engagement between her and her business associates. In addition, by acknowledging her feelings, she recognized a pattern of putting "too many eggs in one business basket," which motivated her to develop and implement a proactive rather than reactive business strategy, and allowed her to diversify her business offerings and relationships.

Wright

So what you're saying here is that uncomfortable emotions have the potential to provide added value to the situation once they're brought out into the open, right?

DeMers

If done in a constructive way, absolutely! And this is applicable to more than just uncomfortable emotions. Wonderful feelings are also powerful drivers for success. Both are loaded with important energy and information. The trick and the challenge are to bring them to the light of day within a supportive framework so that they can be leveraged proactively rather than defended against reactively.

Wright

What happens when these feelings are kept hidden from view?

DeMers

Anaerobic emotional composting sets in. This occurs when uncomfortable feelings are systematically withheld, avoided, minimized, dismissed, denied, and/or projected onto others rather than openly, honestly, and effectively expressed in the present. With a lid kept on these emotions, a closed or "oxygen starved" emotional environment develops. As with anaerobic organic composting, this slows down the emotional composting process.

Unfortunately, anaerobically composting emotions kept under cover grow old with emotional "mold," feeling progressively worse with time rather than completing the emotional composting process and contributing toward future relationship success. Building resentments, simmering anger, rage, hate, guilt, shame, inadequacy, depression, chronic anxiety, worry, frustration, burnout, fear, mistrust, and stress all reflect anaerobic emotional composting in action.

As these buried emotions begin to take on a life of their own, increasing amounts of time, energy, and resources are needed to help keep them under control while at the same time maintaining an outward veneer of emotional well being. The behaviors, roles, and strategies used may work well in the short-term, but over the long-term they become increasingly unsustainable.

For example, a well-intentioned healthcare professional, driven by a sincere desire to help others (as well as by core feelings of guilt, inadequacy, and abandonment) had historically taken on caseloads of heroic proportions. Initially he was seen as a rising star in the healthcare profession, with accolades given by his peers and supervisors giving him the emotional lift that he was seeking.

Twelve years into his career, he found himself exhausted, stressed out, and burned out, overwhelmed by the insatiable demands of the healthcare system, and a growing sense of despair within. Rather than airing out his emotional angst to others, he continued to internalize his feelings and began abusing prescription drugs as a means to maintain an emotionally stable bottom line. Five years later, he was caught in the throes of a full-blown drug addiction, which severely hindered his judgment, effectiveness, and performance at work. Because of violating professional and ethical standards, he lost both his job and his license to practice.

Medical professionals believe that over 90 percent of diseases in the world today are caused by stress! From an emotional composting perspective, it could be said that anaerobically composting emotions, or what I would term "emotional pollution," is the primary culprit. Not so surprisingly, the word "disease," when separated into its two syllables, spells *dis*-ease. A mindset, relationship, groupthink, culture, and/or society in which anaerobic emotional composting prevails is a sure-fire way to create dis-ease.

In addition to causing illness, dis-ease will ultimately drive people apart. Marriage is a powerful example of this because at least half of all marriages will eventually end up in divorce. In my former psychotherapy practice, I observed that most couples coming through the door were locked in conflict because of uncomfortable emotions buried and brooding within their marriage. Not having the awareness, tools, and skills to effectively bring these feelings out into the open, they'd been suffering emotionally and taking their suffering out on each other rather than recognizing what they were truly feeling and leveraging this important information toward the success of their relationship.

When it comes to realizing opportunity for growth, accepting emotional pain as a mandatory part of this process and realizing that emotional suffering is optional is key. As in the gym, if there's no pain, there's no gain. This doesn't mean, however, that one needs to suffer through the workout.

I'm sure you've heard the phrase "the road to hell is paved with good intentions." This is a remarkably insightful statement. According to the *American Heritage Dictionary,* the Indo-European root of the Germanic word *"hel"* (whose Old English meaning is a "black and fiery place of eternal torment for the damned"), is *"kel,"* which means to "cover, conceal." When efforts to sustain personal, professional, relational, business, and corporate well-being are fueled by strategies that cover uncomfortable emotional truths, all hell can break lose. It isn't a matter of being good, bad, right, or wrong—it's just a basic law of emotional composting physics.

Hewlett-Packard's executive board spying scandal in 2006 provides an excellent example of this. Lacking the awareness, tools, skills, and strategies to constructively air out deep-rooted feelings of mistrust, tension, resentment, and animosity festering within the boardroom, board members resorted to reactive behavioral strategies which kept the core emotional issues hidden from view.

While their efforts were well intended, the results were anything but. A series of underhanded, unethical, and illegal behaviors prevailed, eventually spiraling out of control, leading to media scrutiny, congressional inquiry, the dismissal of a number of board members including the chair, a public "black eye" for HP, and a lose-lose for all involved.

Herein lies the power of emotional composting, as it provides a quantum yet practical framework for delivering a return on emotional investment, regardless of how much "hell" these emotions have been through.

Wright

Wow! This sounds like powerful stuff! How did you happen to come across this way of looking at emotions?

DeMers

In retrospect, it has been an amazing confluence of events. In going forward, however, I was simply stumbling through life trying to feel good about myself, and unwittingly heading in the opposite direction. It wasn't until I faced a series of personal, relational, and professional challenges during my late twenties and early thirties when I literally fell into my own emotional composting bin. Neck deep in emotional muck, I had no choice but to make sense of where I landed.

Initially, I realized that I'd only compounded rather than eliminated childhood feelings of insecurity, fear, shame, etc. through various kinds of pleasure, approval-seeking, and emotionally avoidant behaviors as an adult. Only after years of serious soul-searching, counseling, a return to graduate school, getting married, changing careers, opening a psychotherapy practice, working with hundreds of amazing clients, and spending a little time composting organic material in my back yard, was I finally able to complete the connection. Buried emotions never went away—they simply hid beneath the surface, creating an emotional stink as they clamored for attention. If left untended, they'd eventually take on a life of their own, causing all sorts of problems within the very fabric of the relationships in which they were festering.

It was only when these same feelings were invited out into the light of day within a safe, supportive, and non-judgmental framework, or what I would term an emotional composting bin, that their inherent value could be finally be seen, experienced, and leveraged for the greater good of all concerned.

Wright

You mentioned an emotional composting bin. What exactly is that?

DeMers

Metaphorically speaking, an emotional composting bin is an invisible framework inherently built into any and all relationships (whether with one's self, within marriage, family, among friends, co-workers, organizations, management teams, executive boards, business cultures, etc.) through which emotions are expressed. In essence, the relationship is the bin.

Since the dynamics of every relationship are different, how effectively emotions are composted will vary from relationship to relationship and from one context to another. Relationships that compost the most effectively are those whose participants bring high levels of *THREE* to the table. *THREE* stands for:

- Trust
- Honesty
- Respect for self and others
- Emotional awareness
- Effective emotional expression

When these factors remain high, emotions experienced within the relationship easily flow through it, energizing participants in the short-term, and allowing the relationship to flourish in the long-term. When these factors remain low, emotional pressure and toxicity build, reducing relationship efficiency and performance, and increasing relationship dysfunction. Without intervention, the relationship ultimately derails. Low levels of *THREE* create instability (or in some cases, insaneability), while high *THREE* values create sustainability.

It's worth noting that if any of these values are low (i.e., very little trust or honesty in the relationship), then the ability of the relationship to compost emotions effectively is severely compromised. This is because trust, honesty, respect, emotional awareness, and effective emotional expression are interdependent, mutually inclusive, and synergistic in nature.

Trust is the foundational component of an emotional composting bin. Metaphorically speaking, trust is like an invisible layer of ice that supports emotional honesty within the relationship. Should the ice be too thin, however, certain emotions may lack critical support, break through, and slip beneath the surface. Trapped underneath in survival mode, these feelings have no choice but to begin composting anaerobically, which will only further destabilize the relationship.

Without a solid foundation of trust, an extraordinary amount of energy may be needed to sustain relationship performance. The late John O. Whitney, former director of the Deming Center for Quality Management, identified that 50 percent of time in business is wasted because of lack of trust. This is a compelling statistic!

On the other hand, a solid foundation of trust naturally invites and supports emotional honesty. Depending on the situation and circumstance, this trust can be provided by others, and it can be brought forward from within.

Infants provide powerful examples of this. Born with the innate ability to trust their parents completely, infants are ready, willing, and able to freely and openly express their emotions. It may not always look pretty, but it's marvelously effective in helping them process information, get their needs met, bond emotionally with their parents, and ground them in the here and now.

For parents, this presents a wonderful opportunity to respond to these very raw and powerful emotions in proactive, responsive, and nurturing ways rather than to react defensively against them. If parents are attentive, open, and patient with this process, they'll discover a profound method to this madness. As any parent knows though, it's easier said than done.

Wright

Would it be fair to say that children, by being so open and honest with their feelings, have something important to teach their parents?

DeMers

You're right on the mark. Children, by their very nature, constantly give their parents powerful opportunities to become much more attuned to both the very best and worst of their own emotions. In the best of scenarios, these emotions can be composted and leveraged toward the growth and success of the entire family. It is, however, a life-long process filled with many ups and downs, struggles, and challenges.

Albert Einstein once commented that God always uses the simplest way. Framed within the context of emotional composting, children's unadulterated pathways of emotional expression provide a powerfully direct route toward seeing the bigger picture, should their parents be open to this possibility.

Wright

Very interesting! What about honesty and respect? How do they play a part in this process?

DeMers

Being honest simply means telling the truth. Honesty brings "oxygen" into the relationship just as turning the compost pile over brings oxygen into the composting process.

Being respectful maximizes the effectiveness of being honest, while avoiding the pitfalls of being overly, brutally, inappropriately, and/or reactively honest. This is done by recognizing the limitations and strengths of the relationship, how well it supports honesty, and by optimizing the timing and context of what will be said.

For example, if a husband is overwhelmed by financial concerns in his marriage, it's probably not a good idea to bring this up while shopping at Neiman Marcus with his wife. Rather than risk emotional fall-out, this conversation would be better undertaken at a neutral place and another time.

The same holds true in the business setting. If a sales rep makes a mistake on an important business account, rather than being called out on the carpet in front of others, the sales manager would better establish respect by scheduling a constructive conversation in private, behind closed doors. Solid boundaries provide a framework of support, which respects the emotional content of the relationship and maximizes emotional composting efficiency.

Wright

How does emotional awareness influence the effectiveness of the emotional composting bin?

DeMers

If one is emotionally unaware, the majority of information available in the moment will be missed. As a result, critical information could be lacking as part of one's decision-making process. In a very real sense it's like flying blind.

I once had a client who stated he had no emotions. His lack of emotional awareness had prevented him from recognizing the fact that he was experiencing a tremendous amount of stress and anxiety in his life, which was negatively impacting his business, driving his marriage apart, and affecting his overall health. He was just too busy to notice.

Being emotionally aware requires the willingness to slow down, tune in, and recognize the flow of emotions within, as well as the emotions being expressed by those around us. For many folks, this can be a daunting challenge, as the driven quality of their lives forces them to skim quickly across the surface of their emotional selves rather than allowing them to dive in more deeply. In addition, people can easily confuse the intensity of their lives with emotional intimacy.

Nonetheless, with some time, effort, and commitment, this can easily be accomplished. Deep breathing, prayer, meditation, journaling, reflective time alone, eating well, exercise, a good night's sleep, spending time in nature, investing time with children, and honest dialogue with others are all simple yet powerful ways to improve emotional awareness. In addition, emotional upheavals caused by significant personal, relational, professional, and business successes, crises, and/or events always afford valuable opportunities to become more emotionally attuned to self and others.

Wright

When one becomes aware of what he or she is feeling, what happens next?

DeMers

This is where effective emotional expression comes into play. This consists of harnessing, taking ownership of, and leveraging one's emotions toward the greater good of the relationship. Since emotions are such powerful, dynamic, and often unpredictable forces, a great deal of flexibility, creativity, insight, balance, courage, and discipline is required in order to do this well. Consider the following:

- Emotions contain much bigger chunks of information than our thoughts do and therefore, can easily overwhelm the pathways by which we normally express ourselves. This can lead to thinking, behaving, and reacting *against* our emotions rather than thinking, behaving, and expressing ourselves in alignment *with* our emotions.

- We can feel vulnerable and out of control when uncomfortable emotions emerge. Rather than risk this, it's much easier to keep a lid on them.

- Negative feelings about our feelings (e.g., feeling guilty for feeling overwhelmed or feeling embarrassed for feeling sad) can compound our emotional discomfort and interfere with expressing emotions effectively.

- Negative beliefs about our feelings (e.g., I shouldn't be feeling this way or real men aren't supposed to cry) can also compound our emotional discomfort and further derail this process.

- We fear negative consequences of being emotional (e.g., I might be fired if I let my boss know I'm upset or if I let her know that I'm angry—it will ruin the whole evening).

- Cultural norms, expectations, and values don't support a broad range of open and honest emotional expression.

- We lack the words, skills, tools, awareness, and/or role models to effectively articulate our feelings.

Because of these factors, effective emotional expression tends to run against the grain of how most adults communicate, especially when uncomfortable emotions come into play. Some of the following suggestions may be of help in improving emotional expression for those unaccustomed to going with their own emotional flow:

- When uncomfortable emotions emerge, using "I feel" statements, such as "I feel confused," "I feel overwhelmed," or "I feel mistrustful" allows for ownership of these feelings, brings fresh air into the situation and/or relationship, and provides room to leverage these feelings proactively, rather than react against them defensively

- Honest expression of thought improves effective emotional expression. By honestly voicing your thoughts, you contribute to the process.

- Not every feeling (or thought) needs to be acknowledged or expressed. During the course of the day, most emotions naturally flow through our activities and conversations, and are composted and recycled as a result.

- Emotions that are repeatedly ignored or allowed to build up over time are those that become the most toxic and ultimately derail the relationship. Identifying what these feelings are, when they occur, and developing and executing strategies that will allow them to be effectively expressed will reverse this cycle and improve relationship performance.

- Knowing what your Emotional Hot Potatoes (EHPs) are will make a difference. These are emotions that seem too hot to handle and get tossed aside or at others rather than directly acknowledged and expressed. Some people are extremely uncomfortable with feelings of embarrassment, others with resentment, still others with anger. Identifying your personal EHPs, the situations in which they occur, how they might add value if acknowledged, and steps that can be taken to effectively handle and manage them, will help cool them down and make them leveragable.

- Some emotions need to "percolate" rather than be expressed in order to be composted. Sometimes a long walk, a good workout, or a restful night's sleep rather than a long drawn out discussion will do the trick.
- Taking action after achieving emotional clarity is of essence. Emotional compost works best when leveraged forward rather than left behind.

In summary, relationship strategies based on developing high levels of trust, respect, honesty, emotional awareness, and effective emotional expression insure an optimal balance of *THREE* and become powerful catalysts for relationship sustainability and success.

Wright

Given that emotions are an integral part of our lives, who would best benefit from emotional composting?

DeMers

Since this is a process rather than an event, those who'd benefit the most would be individuals, couples, businesses, and organizations that value and are committed to creating meaningful and sustainable positive change rather than those seeking short-term quick fixes. In addition, the willingness and courage to become comfortably uncomfortable with uncomfortable emotions are of essence.

Individuals utilizing this framework have a powerful opportunity to develop emotional honesty and intimacy with themselves, and leverage this information toward identifying and fulfilling their deepest passions, career aspirations, and life-long goals. This also provides the opportunity to develop proactive and sustainable strategies with which to generate success, significance, and meaning in their lives. Benefits would also include improved emotional intelligence, enhanced relationship skills, better health, reduced stress, improved focus, insight, and clarity, and a life-long creative spark.

Given that marriage is such a powerful purveyor of emotions—including the good, the bad, and the ugly—a fully functional emotional composting bin is essential for the success of any marriage. Marriage is about growth, change, and transformation; having a fully functional bin in place makes all of this possible. Without a framework to effectively contain, compost, and leverage the wealth of emotions that marriage brings forth, dysfunction, derailment, and divorce become highly likely.

For small to mid-sized business, emotional composting provides a simple yet effective framework with which to improve culture, optimize employee relations, improve customer service, spark creativity, drive innovation, develop leaders, build more effective teams, manage change more effectively, and improve business strategy.

In a corporate setting, emotional composting offers a means for senior leaders and executives to improve emotional intelligence, enhance communication and interpersonal skills, develop more effective conflict resolution strategies, improve thought leadership capabilities, improve strategic planning, assist in team-building efforts, improve decision-making skills, align values and actions with mission, and enhance overall corporate culture.

As an ethical decision-making tool, emotional composting provides a compelling financial argument for use in the executive board. Recently, executives at Purdue Pharma were fined $634 million for providing misleading information about the drug Oxycontin, and Merck & Co. agreed to pay out a whopping $4.85 billion to settle lawsuits stemming from unethical business practices. If a decision-making strategy promoting trust, honesty, respect, emotional awareness, and effective emotional expression were leveraged across the board in all corporate cultures, the benefit to the bottom line would be staggering. Not only is emotional compost recyclable and leveragable, it is profitable.

In many important ways, emotional composting, with its focus on creating relational sustainability, parallels emerging initiatives driven by business, government, and society, which promote environmental sustainability. Emotional composting provides a simple, yet powerfully effective paradigm that leverages the right emotional solution as a means to eliminate emotional pollution.

Wright

So in closing let me ask you, what might be a next "first step" that the reader might take to begin making emotional composting an integral part of his or her life?

DeMers

I would suggest pausing for a moment, closing your eyes, taking at least ten slow, deep breaths, and identifying *exactly* what you're feeling right now in *this* moment. Write this down and then ask yourself two questions: "What are my feelings telling me?" and "How can I best leverage this information to my advantage?" After you've arrived at an answer, identify an action step that you will take *today* that makes use of this information, and commit yourself to executing this action step before the day is done. This should be more than enough to get you on the right track.

Wright

I really appreciate the time you've taken here to answer all these questions. I've found this whole topic to be interesting and simple, but important. And you have made it very, very clear to me and I'm sure to the readers as to how to understand this subject. It's been extremely interesting.

DeMers

Thank you very much, David. It's been a pleasure!

About Bob DeMers...

BOB DEMERS is the founder and principal of Coaching Works, a relationship-driven and results-orientated coaching, consulting, organizational, and leadership development firm in Charlotte, North Carolina. As a Certified Professional Coach, Certified Mediator, Licensed Clinical Professional Counselor (LCPC), Licensed Alcohol and Drug Counselor (LADC), former television meteorologist, and long-term business owner, he brings wide-ranging professional expertise and life experience in helping his clients elevate their levels of  personal, professional, relational, and business success. Bob is an active member of the Charlotte Chamber of Commerce, Lake Norman Chamber of Commerce, International Coach Federation, Charlotte Area Chapter of International Coach Federation, Charlotte Area Chapter of the Society of Human Resource Management, and Rotary International. Being passionate about a great many things, including his family, music, weather, the Boston Red Sox, and sharing the best of what he's learned about life with others, Bob is currently authoring the first in a series of books, *Emotional Composting*™ *101*, a practical, insightful, and intriguingly quantum perspective on emotions and how to effectively harness and leverage this powerfully creative energy toward achieving personal, professional, relational, and business success.

Bob DeMers
Coaching Works
212 South Tryon Street, Suite 1680
Charlotte, NC 28281
Phone: 704.731.5670
Fax: 704.375.0756
E-mail: bobdemers@coaching-works.net
www.coaching-works.net

Chapter Fourteen

An interview with...

Carl Casanova

David Wright (Wright)

Carl Casanova is a highly sought-after success coach, seminar leader, author and facilitator. He has made it his life work to assist individuals and businesses reach maximum levels of empowerment and success. He is a leading expert in providing professional development and personal growth to entrepreneurs, professionals and organizations that are ready for transformation. He holds a Master of Science Degree in counseling psychology from Oregon State University. As well as founding THE CENTRE, a school for executive training, personal development, and coach certification (ICF), he is an adjunct college professor teaching communication and business classes. He is renowned for his passion and motivational style and his message is geared to inspire personal and professional development. Carl is also the author of the book "What Every Successful Person Knows" and has presented on numerous radio and TV appearances.

Today we are talking about an important chapter in our book entitled *Celebration*. Carl, welcome to *Blueprint to Success!*

Carl Casanova (Casanova)

Thank you so much, thank you for having me!

Wright

So, what is celebration?

Casanova

First and foremost, let me say celebration is a beautiful thing. It is something we each need more in our lives today. We live longer, happier, and healthier when we incorporate more celebration. A lot of people see celebration from different perspectives, but from my perspective celebration is the act of a festivity. It's the act of appreciation; it's the act of gathering to create a feeling of enjoyment and confirmation. Celebration is a verb. It's action, it's a behavior, and it's something you do to make a statement. Visualize yourself sitting in a coffee shop. All of a sudden someone stands up and yells, "Hey people, come on, let's celebrate!" The probable response would be people pausing, looking at each other and all of a sudden joining in. Now there is movement; people start raising their hands, smiling and sharing good vibrations. It brings forth connection, music, eating, gifts, dancing, fireworks—or maybe it's just sitting by yourself after you've accomplished a goal or something significant and just sipping on a latte from Starbucks and saying yes, "it's finished!" Time to relax. It could be as simple as that. One way I personally enjoy celebrating is by visiting a bookstore and purchasing a new book for myself. Celebrating is expressed in many ways and means many things to many different people. It's certainly something that we need more of, possibly just to reduce stress and anxiety, less depression and breakdowns, and experience a greater sense of living life to its fullest.

Wright

How does the act of celebrating bring about benefits?

Casanova

The benefits of celebration are numerous. Celebration is about people. It brings forth the positive in what people are doing and accomplishing. It is acknowledging that something is being completed or about to start and you're creating recognition and sharing the benefit of making it a good and memorable time.

Besides uplifting feelings and sharing with others, celebration brings forth a real sense of affirmation that you experience within yourself. It says that you have worked hard or created something special and here you are at an empowering place, and it's time to shout, "Let's throw a party." It says "Thank you" to others, to life, to yourself, to God, and to living. It is an expression of gratitude and thanksgiving so that in its self is a huge benefit. Imagine what our world would be like if we spent more time being grateful and thankful. Imagine the benefits to our children, our community and to everyone. Never underestimate the many benefits of celebration.

Wright

How has celebrating been a part of our culture?

Casanova

It is a special and important part of our culture here in the USA and has been for years. We seem to be mindful of the big celebrations. Take for example the 4ᵗ of July. What a celebration in our society! People gather together with families for barbeques, games, conversation, fireworks and celebrate something that has historical significance to our country. We gained independence and freedom, so we celebrate.

However, we also celebrate in a lot of different ways and for various causes. It is common in our culture to celebrate birthdays, graduations, marriages, the birth of a newborn, anniversaries, religious holidays and other events. Throughout the year something or someone is celebrating somewhere; so there are a lot of different reasons and ways that our culture celebrates. We really are a society that celebrates and our history of celebration definitely has deep roots. The ancient Greeks, the Athenians, culture of 2500 years ago use to celebrate over 50 holidays and all sporting events throughout the year. The entire city of Athens, a population of 75,000, would close down and everyone would participate in the celebration. There are also small ways to celebrate. As a success coach I often recommend field work activities for my clients to enhance their success. When completed we brainstorm on creative ways to celebrate that achievement. It anchors the growth and the affirming feelings of accomplishment.

Wright

This culture is always thinking about what is and is not appropriate. When and where is the best time to celebrate?

Casanova

I believe that any time is a time to celebrate and when and where is really up to the individual. Your creative imagination really must come forth to live a celebratory life. It is really a worthwhile cause to make celebration a constant in your life. It doesn't have to be formal or even planned. Sometimes just being spontaneous is even better. Getting people together is part of the fun. It could be at a restaurant, it could be at a park, it could be in your living room, it could be in your backyard. There are just a lot of different places where people can gather together to celebrate. It doesn't have to be a perfect time—it doesn't have to be a "perfect" situation or place for celebration to happen. I remember a client once said they love singing in the shower before work. It was a form of celebrating and it helped him get in the mood to start celebrating the day. The law of celebration states that there are ample reasons to create celebration. It's looking for the delight in your life, the joy in living and the desire to share it with others.

Wright

How can a person encourage and cultivate others to celebrate?

Casanova

I think the best way is through example. I remember a specific lady, her name is Miss Drescher, and she's a popular woman at a hair salon called Tangles Hair Salon. Her friends, her customers and her adult children just love being around her. It's like the word is out that if you go and see her, or if you get a haircut from her, it's like a special event and a memorable experience. Once I was in there myself and it's like wow! She creates a celebratory environment with laughter, music, inspiring words and it's with all her customers. It's like you've shifted into a great mood, having fun, celebrating and you just end up feeling good. I asked her where she got this sense of celebration from and she said, "It was my father who was a dentist, and we had five children in the home and it was like he made life a party. He was always entertaining and always creating laughter. He would make mundane situations into special events, even when times were hard." Miss Drescher is always booked weeks in advance at the Tangles hair salon. So the way your being, your personal example, motivation and energy is a perfect model to encourage and cultivate others to celebrate. One only needs to be willing to make life and living a special event and get in the habit of throwing more celebratory parties or attending more. I'm reminded of a saying by the legendary UCLA basketball coach, John Wooden, who said, "Things turn out the best for those who make the best of the way things turn out."

Wright

What will having a celebratory attitude attract into my life?

Casanova

It will attract individuals who want to have and be a part of that inspiring, charismatic, outlet. It will attract individuals who want to look at the brighter side of life, possibly look at their cup as *half full* versus half empty. It will attract a sense of community that connects, cares, and has fun. It will attract individuals who will want to say, "You know, I want to have what that person has." It will encourage others to look for something to celebrate. It will motivate others to look deeper into their own personal life and find something to be happy about and share it with others. I would much rather be with someone who knows how to celebrate life than with someone who does not. An attitude of celebration can have a ripple effect. Just imagine more happiness, more joy, more laughter, and more people sharing and celebrating life. How great would that be!

Wright

For me celebration is just a release of many kinds of great feelings and uplifting spirit. So what has held people up from living a life of celebration?

Casanova

I believe that there's been a lot of poor modeling concerning the topic of celebration and how to celebrate. Much of this goes back to a person's childhood. For many they possibly were not in a home where they saw the value of celebrating. It could have been an environment where it was very rigid, no joy, conditional love, and not a lot of fun. Possibly a limited or no focus on the positives with family members or within the home life. For many adults today their childhood home was a difficult place for them to experience a feeling of celebration. Maybe the hurt was too deep that tapping into the feeling of celebration felt foreign. In many ways it really has held them back now as an adult from living a thrilling and fulfilled life with plenty to celebrate. It's amazing how many issues in our lives go back to our childhood even the ability to celebrate. Many people don't have a knowledge base of how to create celebration or have a consciousness to celebrate. It's like Monday to Friday, then have the weekend, and start all over on Monday. So there's not really a conscious mindset toward celebration in their life. It's easy to get stuck in a rut and lose your sense of balance which celebration certainly is a part of living a well-balanced life. I remember a time in my life when I found myself being centered on work only, and my life was not balanced at all. It created a lot of anxiety, and I found myself often irritated, especially with family and others quite easily. Some time later a friend noticed and said, "Hey, you know there's something wrong here," and I shared what I was going through and this caring friend said, "Carl, it sounds to me that acknowledging and celebrating what you have would really be helpful. Start with stopping to smell the roses!"

My first thought was who's got time to stop and smell roses? How ridiculous is that? I did some serious reflection and considered what that statement really meant. It was to slow down, look at the pleasurable things of life, take a moment to breath and enjoy—I discovered that was exactly what I needed to do. Stop, and smell the roses. And I had no idea that this simple act would actually lower my anxiety and give me a new perspective. It really worked!

Wright

What specific emotions or possible triggers would bring on the spirit of celebration?

Casanova

From my perspective, the specific emotions that often ignite or would trigger bringing on the spirit of celebration would be gratitude, and a feeling of being thankful. For all of us we are looking to find ways to improve our lives and for ways to enhance our total way of being. From all the tough lessons I've learned and the people I've worked with I've discovered it's not until you appreciate the things you have right now that things will really shift in a prosperous direction. I believe the things of the present would mean more to you when you give thanks and appreciate what you've had or didn't have in the past. The times my heart was filled with gratitude were the times I really felt rich with abundance in my life. I also sensed a deeper spiritual and more meaningful connection. Your ability to celebrate life would be much more enriching, purposeful, and appreciative, especially as you move forward toward your future.

Wright

How would you tell our readers to incorporate a greater sense of celebration in life, possibly even in our careers and workplace?

Casanova

I believe your personal life does reflect on your professional life and vise versa. Work is an important part of our lives but it is not our life. I do recognize our life at work can be very stressful. A lot of anxiety comes about with constant deadlines and quotes to meet, sales to make, and often times the breakdown of workplace communication. I encourage people to really find ways to observe how they are living day to day. How healthy are you and are you emotionally, mentally, physically, spiritually, relationally, and socially balanced. Take a good look at your tension level and do you need to reduce stress. Do not make work the primary focus. You've got to have a life; you've got to have something outside of your work that is going to bring you greater meaning and that feeling of high worth. Have an understanding that there's more than just earning an income to pay off bills and advance up the latter. The key is finding happiness and personal purpose. I'm not saying that work is not fulfilling, but programming yourself for a productive life outside of work will actually make your career and work life better. I encourage individuals to incorporate different hobbies. Have a caring and loving support system. Be close to family and friends. Include others who bring different positive attributes that can introduce you to some creative and fun activities. Take classes, take trips, and take some time off just for yourself. If this is difficult, seek a mentor or hire a Life Coach for greater insight and accountability. We all know life is difficult, however it is up to each person to chose how they want to live. Choosing celebration helps the journey to lighten up.

Wright

Did you have any mentors as you came along to think this deeply about celebration? I had one friend that told me that if I was walking down a country road and saw a turtle sitting on top of a fence post I could bet anything that he didn't get up there by himself!

Casanova

I'm a big advocate of mentors and mentoring. I've had several mentors; one significant mentor was my grandfather, Santiago Velez, who was present when I was growing up in Manhattan, New York. He celebrated life by sharing his love and attention. He modeled high respect and care. He was a great mentor who personally coached me and taught me how to celebrate. He was an encourager and inspired others to celebrate every moment, and every conversation while being a sojourner on this planet. He was that type of person to me and to many other people. What a model he was! Now as a success coach, which in many ways has various elements of mentoring, I've found that assisting individuals to grow and transform their life is a responsible and high calling. I assist people in how to set goals, how to create balance, how to have building blocks to get what they want and how to bring forth more celebration. My mission in every coaching conversation is to accentuate the positives and observe areas that are working well to encourage more celebration. I'm finding that many in the wisdom business or the helping profession are teaching and encouraging more people to celebrate. How to celebrate when they've accomplished things whether big or small. My intention is to be in a constant state of encouraging my students and the people I work with individually or in workshop settings to have that spirit of celebration in all things. Increase celebrating life while you have life to celebrate! What I've heard from people who are in their more senior years of living is, "Gosh, I wish I would have spent more time having fun! More time celebrating, more time with my wife or husband, my son or daughter, going fishing or to sporting events or whatever and celebrating the moments together," so it's important to get to that conversation early and encourage people to start celebrating *now* so we don't have to have that discussion later and have any regrets.

Wright

So how can everyday pleasure be focused on celebrating?

Casanova

How wonderful that we do have many pleasurable things in this life and everyday pleasure can be celebrated by adjusting your attitudes, your focus, and your beliefs. Each person can turn on the celebration button because it is a mental program that is operated by you. Get up in the morning and choose the mindset that is passionate and pro-active. It really starts with you making the choice to live a life that you want to create and have more celebrative events in it. It will make a difference. Some people wake up in the morning and they say, "Oh God, it's morning…" and some people wake up and say, "Thank you, God, it *is* morning!" So much of what takes place depends on how you adjust yourself. How you empower yourself, how you reframe your approaches, and how you utilize your language. You are very much in control of how you want to celebrate your life and how you decide to carry out your days, months, and years. Why not make living enjoyable and pleasurable. Take a break throughout your day to focus on a way to celebrate the moments, the situations, the occasions, on just about anything your heart, mind, or spirit leads you to celebrate. There are times when I'm in my hectic busy mode that I have to just stop, take some time to breathe and call my family or call a friend, and I use that as a celebratory moment. I use that as a pleasurable component in my day to celebrate a conversation with somebody I love—somebody I care for and someone who cares for me. So I'll take some time throughout the day to find small pleasures and make it a celebrative event or occasion. Those small pleasurable moments do add up. Try it, you'll live long, be happier and find yourself celebrating life more.

Wright

This has been a really great conversation, Carl; I really do appreciate spending this time this afternoon with you. I sure have learned a lot about celebration, and I'm sure our readers will also! I appreciate you taking this time with me.

Casanova

I appreciate you spending this time on this very important subject as well, and I appreciate what you are doing there at Insight Publishing!

About Carl Casanova...

CARL CASANOVA, M.S., has been in the helping profession his entire career. He is a keynote speaker as well as facilitates for organizations, teams, businesses, and is a coach to executives. A keynote with Carl is truly a learning experience that generates an attitude shift and maximizes life and work performance. He is renowned for his passion and motivational style. His message is empowering and inspires personal and professional growth. As well as founding THE CENTRE, founded in 2001, a post secondary school for training and certifying executive and life coaches (ICF), as well as personal development. He is an adjunct college professor teaching communication and business classes. Carl's life work is educating others to achieve optimal growth and ongoing success in all areas of life.

Carl Casanova
The Centre
516 SE Morrison, Suite LL2
Portland, OR 97214
503-233-9983
carl@centreforcoachtraining.com
www.thecentreusa.com

Carl Casanova